COPYRIGHT

© **KASPER B. LANGMAN 2022**

All rights reserved. No part of this publication may be reproduced, stored in a retrieval system, or transmitted in any form or by any means, electronic, mechanical, photocopying, recording, or otherwise, without prior written permission of the author.

Printed in the United States of America

CONTENTS

COPYRIGHT	I
CONTENTS	II
CHAPTER 1	1
INRODUCTION TO COMPUTERS	1
What is Operating System?	2
Windows Computers You can Buy	3
Computer Terminology	3
Common Windows Computers	15
How to Setup Your Computer	15
CHAPTER 2	22
LEARNING THE BASICS	22
Mastering Your Computer Keyboard	24
Connecting Your PC to the Internet	34
How to Connect Your Computer to the Internet Using Wi-Fi	35
Connecting Your Computer to Internet Through USB Tethering	38
How to Connect Your Computer to the Internet Using Modem	44
The Desktop of a Windows Computer	46
Creating Folders on the Desktop of a Computer	47
Working with Applications	50
How to Access Apps Installed on Your Computer	50
Getting New Apps in Your Computer	55
CHAPTER 3	65
COMPLETING MORE TASKS IN COMPUTER	65

Apps at the Taskbar by Default 66

Pinning Apps to the Taskbar 74

The Basic Folders 77

How to Create Subfolders inside a Main Folder 79

Copy, Paste and Cut 83

Adjusting Computer Screen Brightness, Flight Mode, Night Light, Battery, Keyboard Layout, Accessibility and Volume 84

Screen Brightness, Volume, and Focus Assist in Windows 10 Computers 88

Surfing the Internet with Web Browser 90
   Accessing the History in a Web Browser 92
   How to Add a Website to Bookmark 94
   Pinning a Web Page to the Taskbar of Your Computer 96
   How to Share a Web Page with Others 98
   How to Print a Webpage 98
   Accessing the Settings of Your Web Browser 98

The Use of Email 102
   How to Signup for a New Email Address 102
   How to Communicate with Your Email Address 106
   Things to Know After Creating an Email Account 109

How to Change a Computer's Name 109

CHAPTER 4   111

MICROSOFT WORD USER GUIDE   111

Launching Microsoft Word 111

Working Smart in Your Document 114

Making Text Bold 115

Capitalizing Words in a Word Document 116

How to Insert Pictures in Word 117
   How to Resize Pictures 119

How to Underline Words 120

Finding Out the Words Count in a Document	120
Changing Font Styles in Document	121
How to Change Text Size	123
How to Save a Document	124
How to Print a Document	125

CHAPTER 5 — 129

GUIDE ON MICROSOFT EXCEL — 129

Excel Terms	131
Launching Excel App for the First Time	134
How to Enter Data in a Spreadsheet	137
How to Make Text Bold in Excel	138
How to Extend a Cell in Excel	139
Changing Text Color in Excel	140
Selecting Spreadsheet Data	141
Creating More than One Sheet in a Workbook	141
Merging Cells of a Spreadsheet	142
Plotting Charts in Excel	144
Printing in Excel	148
How to Save a Workbook	150

APPRECIATION — 152

INDEX — 153

CHAPTER 1

INRODUCTION TO COMPUTERS

Computer is an important tool as it finds its applications in different areas of our life. Knowing how to use computer will increase your productivity. It will make you to be part of the trend. It is hard to see any company or organization in this 21st century that functions without computer. In fact, it is progressing into families. Time will come when you visit any home without finding functioning computers.

Because of the importance of this device, I decided to create this book. This is a book that will put you through on how to operate computers, preferably Windows computers, which I am using for this teaching. Even if you have not used computer before, this book will walk you through on all the basics you need so that you can operate your computer.

If you are a senior who rely on the help of your grandchildren to be able to complete few tasks in your computer, the time has come for you to learn computer and perform those tasks by yourself. After learning from this guide, that your office work will be made easy. It is a Do-It-Yourself book. I will make sure all those common tasks that you can perform with your computer to make you up and running is explained in this book.

Are you a beginner who has a computer but do not know how to use it? It happens sometimes, but I am here to guide you. You will be able to navigate through your computer easily after reading and practicing through this book. In August 2021, a non-academic staff of one university met me on my visit to the school and explained that she has a computer but does not know how to make use of it. She asked that I should teach her on how to use the computer. She is a senior and I was able to put her through.

In fact, that is one of the reasons I composed this book so that both beginners and seniors can learn.

As I stated earlier, this teaching on how you can use computer, and become an expert in it with time is illustrated using Windows Operating System computer. I chose Windows computer because it has the highest number of users globally. In the United States of America alone, 75% of computer users have their computers running Windows OS. With this large proportion, you as a reader of this book is likely to be using the same OS on your computer. Know that the abbreviation **OS** stands for Operating System.

What is Operating System?

I know you might have heard about the term "Operating System" for a long time now. It is a common term used in computer. Because this book is for beginners in computer as well as for seniors, let me throw some light on the term. An Operating System is a software that is installed in a computer before it is sold out for use, and it controls how the computer works and the applications that are installed in that computer. No computer can function without an Operating System. It is the fundamental part of computer that impacts in everything that takes place in the machine.

There are some popular Operating Systems that are installed in different computers. These Operating Systems are as follow:

- Windows Operating System developed and owned by Microsoft
- MacOS developed and owned by Apple
- Linux Operating System developed as Community contributors

These three main Operation Systems used on computers are listed in order of their market shares. Windows OS has more than 75% of the share, followed by MacOS with about 17.72% and lastly Linux OS with market share of about 1.73%. With these statistics, you can see that the Operating System pioneered by the many times world richest man – Bill Gates, has the highest market share. If you have not bought any computer before now, I recommend you go for computers that function with Windows Operating System. One of the reasons is because you will find more materials that will put you through on things that go on in Windows computers when compared with the other two Operating Systems. I like Windows computers, so go for them. That will make your learning from this book smooth. If you can even get the one running the current Windows OS version, Windows 11, that will be much better. Let me go on and guide you on some computers you can buy which will make you more productive.

Windows Computers You can Buy

There are a lot of Windows computers that are available in different marketplaces. Even on Amazon.com website, there are many of them. So, go for any of these Windows computers:

- Microsoft Surface Laptop Studio which sells at about $1494
- HP ENVY 13 which sells at about $849
- Microsoft Surface Laptop Go which sells at about $400
- ASUS VivoBook 15 which sells at about $490
- Lenovo IdeaPad 3 (17 inch) which sells at about $650
- HP Laptop 15 which sells at about $510
- Lenovo IdeaPad 1 which sells at about 370
- HP 17 which sells at about $575
- Acer Swift 3 which sells at about $650

Any of those listed computers is fine if you can get one from the list. But, if you can get any Windows computer that runs Windows 8.1, 10, or Windows 11 version, it is still okay. You will be able to follow adequately with this practical teaching.

Computer Terminology

As someone that wants to learn how to use computer, there are some terms you need to learn. These are the terms that will help you to easily get acquainted to the electronic machine called computer. Yes, computer is an electronic machine. It is defined as an electronic machine that manipulates information fed into it and gives an output, and it is used for storing, retrieving and for processing data. When you feed a computer with information in the language it understands, it gives result based on that information fed into it. Let us return to the main heading under discussion, and that is computer terminology.

Software

Have you heard of software before? What is it about? In computer, software is that part of any computer that you cannot touch. In this teaching, I will be mentioning software often, so, when I say software, I believe you should understand what it is.

Examples of software are those applications that are installed on your computer that you can use to complete specific tasks. Some common software used in computers are Microsoft Word, Microsoft Excel, PowerPoint, calculator software installed on your computer (not that physical calculator you use for Mathematics), and even the Operating System that makes your computer to function. Software is a set of instructions in a computer.

Hardware

As a primary school student, I was taught that a hardware is the opposite of a software. And that teaching is true. Hardware are those components of your computer that you can see, touch and feel. They are not like software that you cannot touch or feel. The plural of hardware is still hardware.

Examples of hardware are keyboard, mouse, monitor and motherboard. All these parts of computer you can see and touch.

From these examples, the only one you may not be able to see without loosing your computer nuts is motherboard. You have to loosen the nuts of your computer before you can see and touch it. But do not do the loosing yourself because you may end up damaging your computer because you are not an expert in that area. If you want to see the motherboard of a computer, go and meet technicians that specialize in computer repair, and they will show one to you.

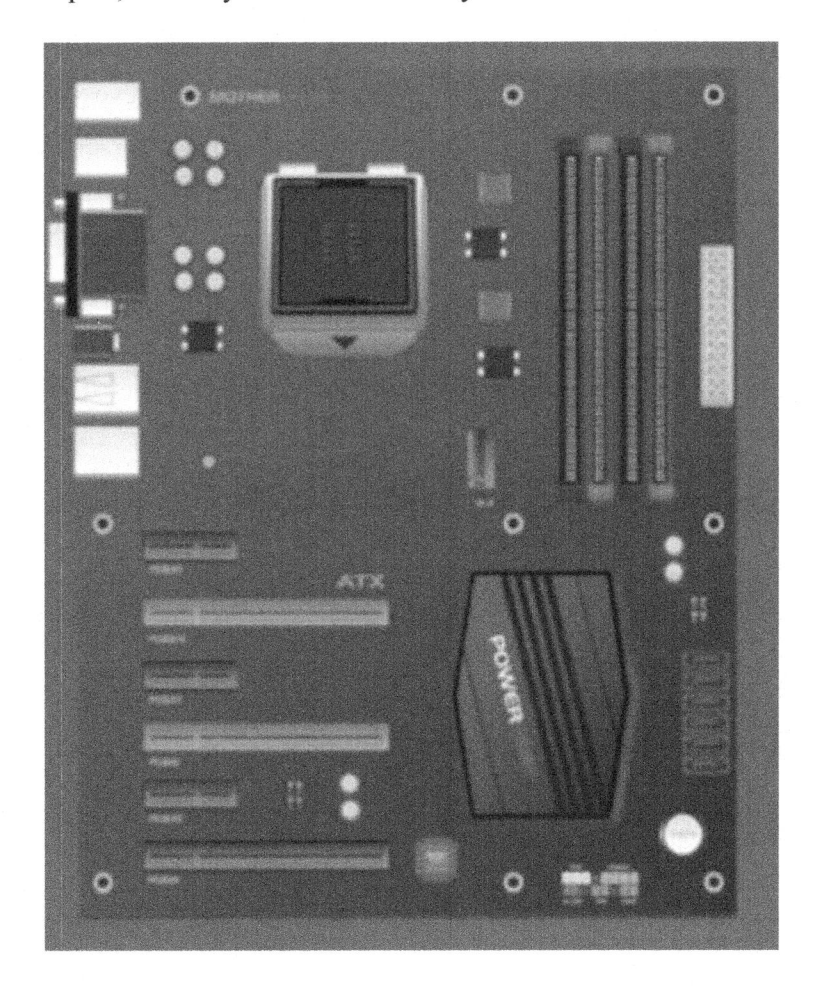

The Motherboard of a computer as an example of a computer hardware

As an added information, the motherboard is the main component of a computer. The RAM, hard disk, and other components of a computer are fixed on a motherboard. As this book is made for beginners and seniors, let me not bore you on other areas of a motherboard. What is important is that at the end of this book, you learn how to operate computer effectively.

Search Bar

A search bar is a space provided in an application which enables users of computers to search for something. A search bar is also called a search space. As a user of Windows computer, you may want to search for something or app in your computer, one of the channels to get to that app can be through the search bar section of your computer. Also, if you are using the browser installed on your computer, you can use the search bar of your computer to search for items on the internet. With this explanation, I believe you know what to do when I instruct you to type a particular text in a search bar. The photo below indicates one of the search bars of Microsoft Edge browser.

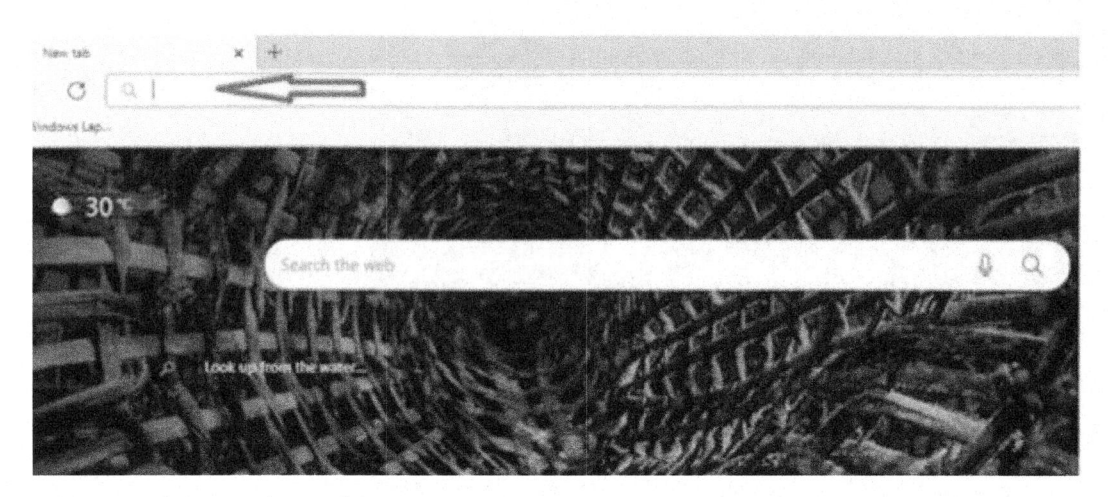

The Search bar indicated by arrow

CPU

In computer, CPU stands for Central Processing Unit. It is an important part of computer. Central Processing Unit is that part of any computer where data is processed. Think of CPU as that part of your computer properties that displays the processor of your computer in the unit of GHZ (Giga Hertz). It determines how fast your computer loads. If you click any command of your computer software and it loads fast, what it means is that the CPU of your computer is a sound one. Experienced computer users consider the CPU of some computers before they make their buying choices.

In addition, Central Processing Unit is the brain of every computer. It is also called the processor of a computer. So, when someone asks you of the CPU of your computer, just understand that he or she is talking about the processor of your computer.

To access the processor of your computer, click the File Explorer of your computer first. The photo below indicates the position of the File Explorer of Windows 11 computer.

The File Explorer of a computer pinned at the taskbar

When the File Explorer opens, look at the right margin of that your computer and you will see a feature named **This PC** or any name your computer is identified with, example KASPER. Click on that **This PC** or the name your computer is identified with, and a new page will open.

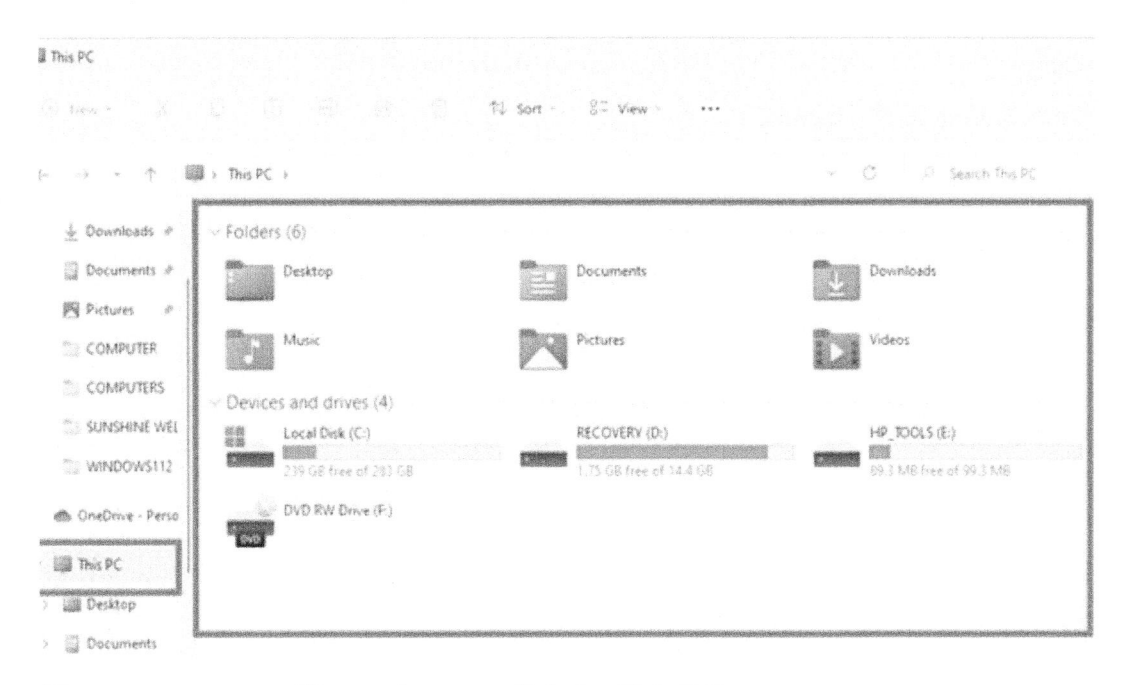

*The new page you will see when you click the **This PC***

7

The next action you are to take is to right-click on an empty page of that This PC page. From the list of options that will be displayed, select **Properties**.

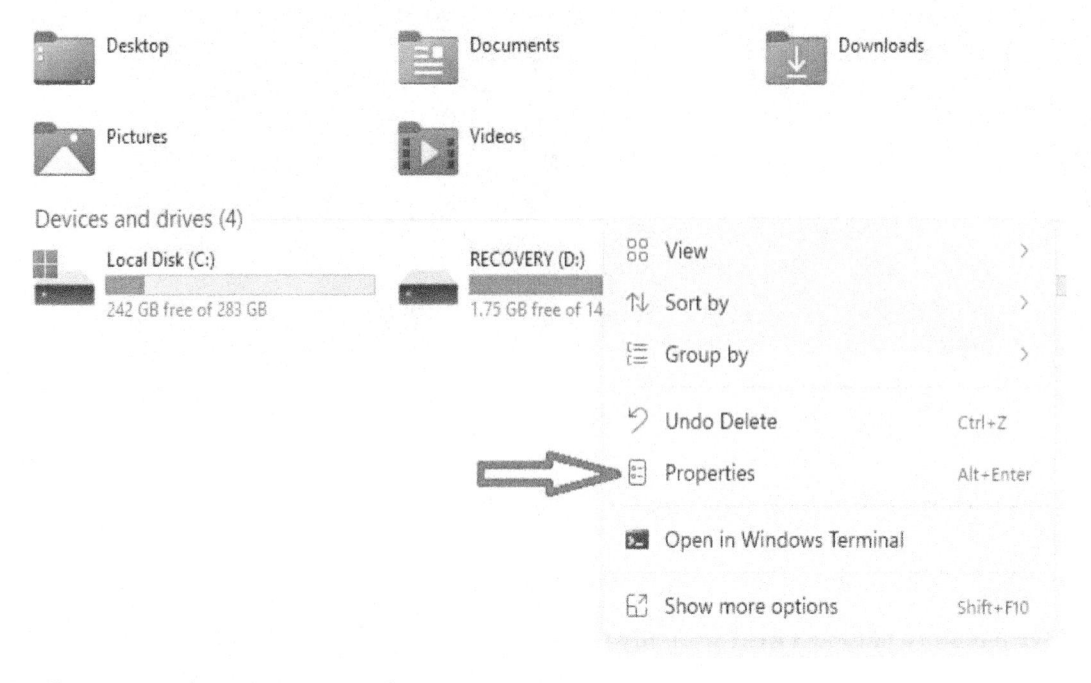

*The **Properties** you are to select*

On taking the above last step, you will see some information about your computer, including the CPU (memory) of the computer. In the photo below, the processor of one of my computers is indicated.

ⓘ Device specifications

Device name	DESKTOP-GNP6HDD
Processor	Intel(R) Core(TM) i3 CPU M 380 @ 2.53GHz 2.53 GHz
Installed RAM	4.00 GB (3.80 GB usable)
Device ID	AE847446-51B2-45D9-85A6-0797D288D31C
Product ID	00325-80000-00000-AAOEM
System type	64-bit operating system, x64-based processor
Pen and touch	No pen or touch input is available for this display

Related links   Domain or workgroup   System protection   Advanced system setting

▉▉ Windows specifications

Edition	Windows 11 Home

The processor information of a computer indicated

Shut down

The term Shut down is a term used in computer which means to power off a computer. So, when someone tells you to shut down your computer, he wants you to switch off that your computer. In computer, it is not that okay you press and hold the power button of your PC before it is powered off. The recommended approach is for you to click the Power button of your computer, and then select **Shut down** option for it to be switched off.

Sleep

Sleep is a computer term. When someone tells you to put your computer into sleep. The person wants you to put your computer in sleep mode. When any computer is placed in a sleep mode, the apps that are opened on the computer are turned to sleep mode and the computer does not do any noticeable work in that state.

To put your Windows computer in a sleep mode, click the **Power button** of the computer, and then select **Sleep** from the options displayed. As soon as you do this, the fan of your computer gradually goes down and the computer is made to sleep.

Hibernate

The Hibernate is another option you will see when you click the Power icon of your computer. The Hibernate makes use of less power when compared to sleep. When you hibernate your computer, all the lights on your computer go off. You are to use this option when you do not want to use your computer for a long hour, and you want to start from where you left off when you return. Assuming you are editing something using your computer and you are called for something that is likely to take more than 4 hours of your time. You can hibernate your computer. In a situation like this, when you return and power on your computer, you can continue your editing because that app you were using for the editing will still be activate.

Restart

The term restart is used in computer just like the others that I explained. When someone tells you to restart your computer, what that person wants you to do is to start your computer again. In some computers, Restart command is replaced with Reboot. Just like Shut down, Sleep and Hibernate, Restart is one of the options you will see when you click the Power button of your computer.

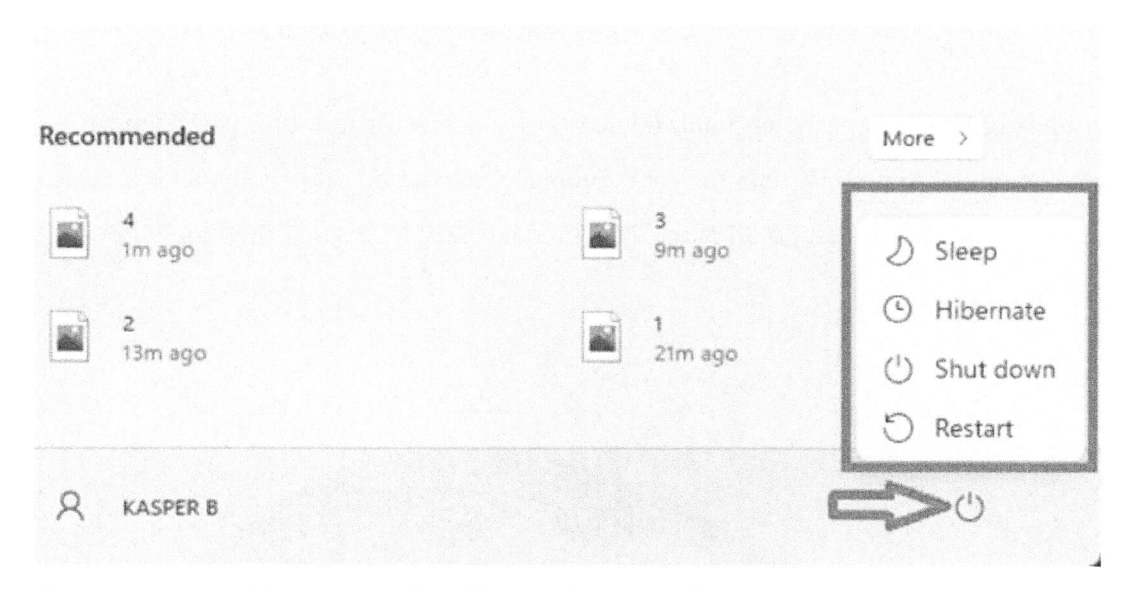

Restart *as one of the commands of Power button*

Why do people restart their computers? In most cases, people restart their computers to make them fast again when they load. If you are working on your computer, and at a point the machine starts to hang, restarting the computer can make it fast again. It may make the computer to be loading faster anytime you click on any command. It is like refreshing the memory of the computer.

RAM

The term RAM stands for Random Access Memory. It is an important part of every computer machine. The size of your computer RAM determines how much opened apps or pages your computer will hold. It is recommended you buy computer that have RAM of 4GB (4 Gigabytes) and above. Any computer that operates with RAM that is less than 4GB may not be able to hold much opened pages. Computers with small RAM size tends to hang when many pages or apps are opened on them. If you are financially okay, go for computers that have big RAM size. It will make you to enjoy the use of computer. In computer, information is stored temporarily in a RAM, and that is the reason RAM is known as a temporary notepad. It is a place where your machine sends some information to the hard disk of your computer.

Input Device

In the world of computer, an input device is any device or tool that you connect into your computer to provide data for your computer to function effectively, and to control signals of the things that go on in the system. An example of a common input device is mouse.

A Mouse as an input device

A computer mouse is a detachable device that when connected to the USB port of a computer or wirelessly connected, is used to make clicks on commands or buttons on computer surface and can also be used for dragging and drop. In summary, mouse is used to control the graphical user interface of any computer. In the absence of mouse device, you can make the control from the touchpad of your computer. That is the reason most laptops do not come with external mouse.

There are other input devices used in computer. They are keyboard, scanner, joystick, camera, microphone, DVD driver and others. These devices all send information into our computers. Keyboard for instance send information into computers and that is the reason any key we press on the keyboard appears on the application being communicated to.

Output Device

As we have input device in computer, so do we have output device as well. As a user of computer for more than 15 years now, I have been interacting with output devices almost every day. In fact, they are always close to me.

The term output device is any tool used in computer that interprets the information fed into it to the way we humans can see, read and understand them. Output devices do great jobs in computer. Examples of output devices are printers, speakers, the monitor of a computer, CD burner, and others. With printer as an output device, the information that we have in Word editors are printed out in hard copy for us to see them clearer and feel them. As the name implies, they bring out the information out to the real world, and hence the name output.

A printer printing out the information that is displayed on computer screen (output)

On the other hand, one of the devices I mentioned as an output device is speaker. I believe you know what speakers do in many electronic devices in our world today. If you have a DVD player in your house or even television, you will know that it is because of the speakers that you can hear the sounds that come out from those electronic devices.

Speakers in computers do the same job. They bring out the sounds that are generate in your computer. Because speakers bring out sounds for we humans to hear in our ears, they are known as output devices.

Keyboard

Keyboard is the part of a computer that contains some keys which you can press to form words or numbers. A keyboard is made up of many keys which can be letters of the alphabet, numbers and symbols. Keyboard is an input device which is modeled after the typewriter of the old days.

The keyboard of a laptop

If you are working with certain applications on your computer, example Microsoft Word, when you press any key of the keyboard, that letter, number, or the special character represent on the keyboard appears in that app. Some keyboards are built into a computer, and some others are detachable. If the inbuilt keyboard of your computer develops fault in the long run, you can buy a detachable one to help you do some works in that your PC. It works fine the same way as the inbuilt keyboard. When I first bought my first laptop, after few years of use, the keyboard of the laptop developed fault.

Because I still like the laptop, I ordered for a detachable keyboard which served me for long.

Common Windows Computers

At the beginning of this book chapter, I mentioned that the teaching in this book will be carried out using Windows computers. This is because Windows computers have the largest market share globally. By Windows computers, I mean the computers that function using Microsoft Windows Operating System. So, if you are using a Windows computer, you are likely to understand this book better and learn faster. The common Windows computers are as follow:

- Any computer produced by Microsoft, example Microsoft Surface Laptop Studio.
- Any computer produced by HP, example HP 630
- Computers manufactured by Lenovo, example IdeaPad Flex 5 (15, AMD)
- Computers manufactured by Dell, example XPS
- Computers manufactured by Acer, example Swift X Intel
- Computers manufactured by ASUS, example ASUS VivoBook 15
- Computers manufactured by LG, example is LG Gram 16

How to Setup Your Computer

Let me assume that a friend or a relation sent a brand-new laptop computer to you, and you do not know how to set it up and configuration. The computer is likely to be a Windows laptop, maybe manufactured by HP, Microsoft, Lenovo, Compact, Acer or any other brand name. You needed a computer and that is the reason that computer is sent to you, or you even bought it with your own money. So, I will guide you on all you need to setup the computer and get it running.

The first step you are to take is to unpack the computer. You are to carefully do that. Use your hand and remove the sellotape that is used to seal the pack that contains the computer. I do not recommend the use of sharp tools like razor blade and knife for the removal of sellotape because it may mistakenly cut through the cables that accompany the PC. When something like this happens, you are likely to feel bad. So, do that removal of the sealing tape with your fingers.

After removal of the seal of the pack, opened the pack and remove the accessories that are in the pack one by one. You are likely to see the charger of the computer first, but it all depends on how the packing was made by the computer manufacturer.

One of the items you will see after removing the contents of the pack is the manual of the computer. You can go through the manual which contains the setup steps of your computer. But do not worry if you do not understand the steps explained in it because that is what I will be teaching you in detail in this subheading.

With the charger of the computer, charge the computer properly. This is because the computer may come with less charge left in the battery. So, charge the computer for at least one hour before you start the setup proper.

After charging of the PC battery, press the Power button of the computer for it to be powered up.

The external Power button of a computer indicated

Depending on the manufacturer of your computer and model, the position of the external Power button of your computer may be different. Irrespective of the position, just press the button for the machine to be powered on. Once you press the Power button, remove your finger from the button and then wait for the screen to appear bright. Because it is the first time of starting up the computer, the power may take longer time to come up.

Once the power comes up, you need to set up the computer step by step. The first thing you may be required to take is to select the region you are at that moment. This is important to the Operating System so that it will know the kind of information to feed you with. The photo below is the screenshot requesting for my location.

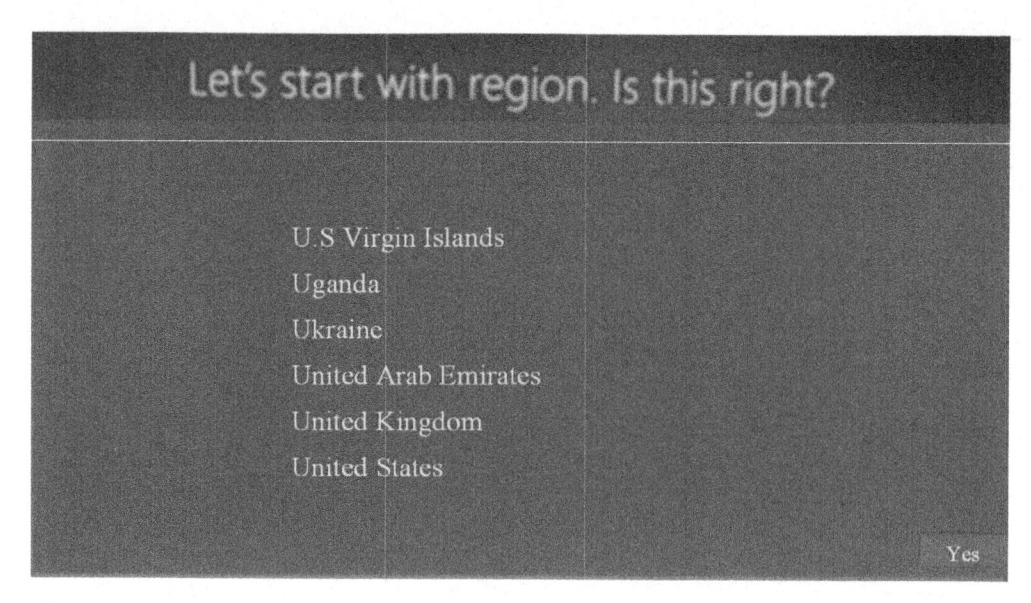

> **Let's start with region. Is this right?**
>
> U.S Virgin Islands
> Uganda
> Ukraine
> United Arab Emirates
> United Kingdom
> United States
>
> Yes

Computer setup in progress – region selection

From the above photo, you can see some countries on the list. If your country is not on the first list of countries, scroll down until you get to your own country, and then click on it.

After clicking on the region you occupy, click **Yes** button. A new page will open. In that new page, you may be required to select keyboard layout of your choice. You may choose the US own or any other you feel comfortable with, and still click **Yes** button which may be positioned at the bottom-right. On clicking the **Yes** button, you may be asked if you need second keyboard layout, just feel free to decide. But in my own case, I did not need any extra keyboard layout.

The next page you will be taken to may be on internet connection. Choose any source of internet you want to use to complete the computer setup. The reason why Windows needs internet network in that stage is so that you can login into your Microsoft account. If you do not have any Microsoft account at that point, you will be guided on how to create one for yourself. But if you do not have any internet access at that point, click the option with **I don't have the internet**. This action will take you to a new page to continue the setup.

On the next page, you may be given some information on why you need to get your computer connect to the internet. But if you still do not have internet at that moment, just skip that section.

On a new page, you need to agree with the Operating System terms and conditions. And for you to accept to the terms and conditions stated on that page, click the **Accept** button. We then keep moving.

On the next page that will open, you may be asked on who is going to use that your PC. The photo below indicates that.

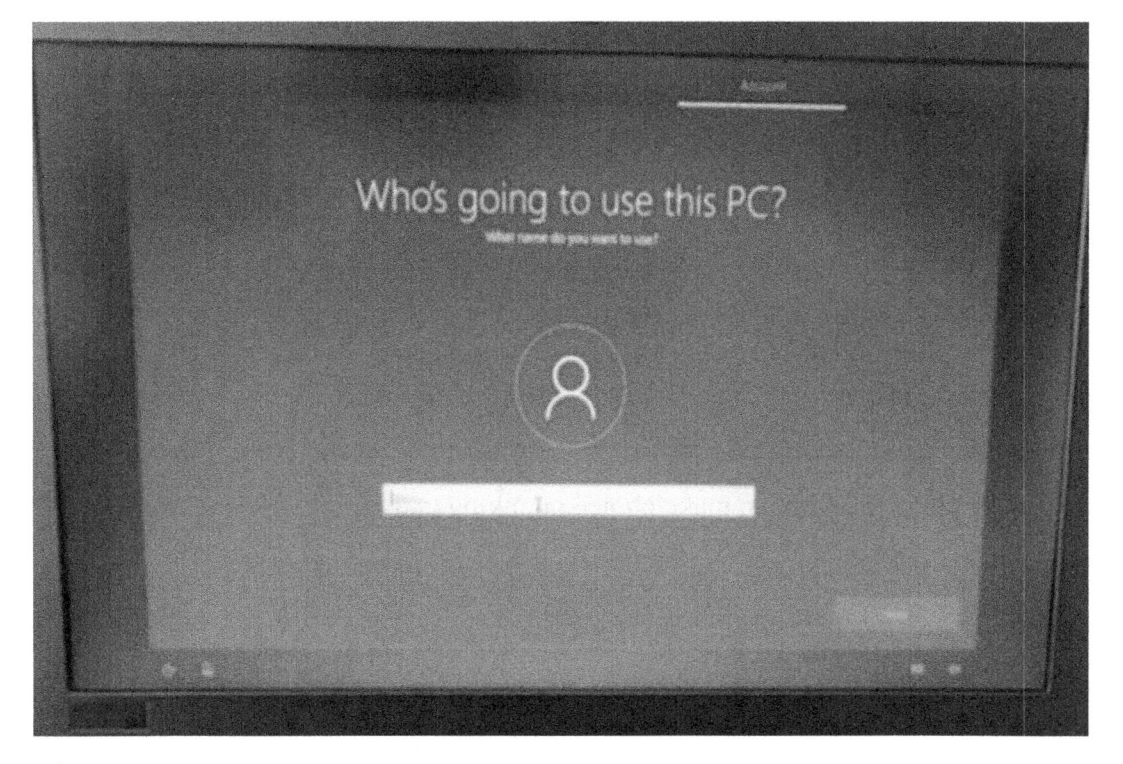

About to give name to a computer

What you are required to do is to give your computer name. So, you can type your name in the space provided, example "Smart G". Know that irrespective of the name you give you computer at the setup stage, you can still change the name to another in future. I will guide you on how to change the name of your computer in a later chapter. After typing the name you want your PC to be identified with, click the **Next** button.

On the next page you will be taken to, you may be required to insert the password you will be using to unlock your computer anytime you want to have access into it. That is security. Microsoft does not play with security because they understand its importance. So, type any password that you know you will easily remember for unlocking of your computer, and then click the **Next** button.

On a new page that will appear right before you, you may be asked if you want the activity history of your computer to be tracked. You will be left with Yes or No answer. Anyone you choose is fine. On giving your answer, you are moved to a new page.

You may be asked if you want to use voice on your computer. This can be translation of voice to text in your computer. Just accept or reject, and then move on with your setup.

Location consent may be the next page you will see. On that page, you will be asked if you want Microsoft and Apps installed on your computer to use your location. You are to click on **Yes** or **No**. In my own time, I selected **No**.

Another page you may see is the find my device setup page. To me, I choose the no option because my computer is always in my home. On making your choice, you are likely to be taken to a page to make choice on inking and typing. Choose from the two options that are displayed before you and then proceed to the next page.

On a new page, you may be required to give your consent on whether you want to get tailored experiences with diagnostic data. During my own setup, I chose no because it was not necessary to me.

The next thing you may see is the App use advertising ID. To me, that is not necessary, and therefore clicked on **No**. App user advertising ID is just an identity assigned to different devices, example computers, to serve adverts on their applications.

You will be landed on device protection page. On this page, you will be required to select your region, your last name and your email address. Fill these details properly because Microsoft wants to use the information for your machine protection. Also, tick some options on how you want that your computer protected. After making the selection and then click the **Next** button, your computer will progress in starting fully. You will see the text that reads **Hi**. Another text you will see will read something like **Just a few moments**. This will be followed by **We're getting everything ready for you**. Just hold on until everything is set.

At the end, everything will be set up properly after some minutes. As it starts, you will see the desktop section of your computer. An example is the one I have as a screenshot below.

The new desktop look of a computer running Windows 11 OS after setup

With this information on how to setup a brand-new Personal Computer, I know you can do it on your own. Just follow the steps presented here. If there is any change in the setup steps of your own computer, it will not be much.

CHAPTER 2

LEARNING THE BASICS

In chapter 1 of this book, I was able to put you through on some things you need to know about computer. I walked you through the explanation of what computer is. I did not stop there but also explained types of computers based on the Operating System that controls the computer. I listed MacOS, Linux computers, Android OS and Windows computer – which has the largest share of the market. That is the reason I am giving my teachings with reference to computers running Windows 11 Operating System.

The computer I am using currently runs Windows 11 OS, and it will be nice you upgrade your own Windows PC to Windows 11 if you are using anything older than the current version. The upgrade is free. So, it will not cost you anything to upgrade your older Windows computer to the latest Windows version. If you need more information on Windows 11 Operating System computers and use, I recommend you buy my book on it. It is on sale on amazon.com.

The book is titled:

"WINDOWS 11 FOR BEGINNERS AND SENIORS 2022: Fully Illustrated User Guide on How to Master Microsoft Windows 11 Operating System.

The front cover image of the book is displayed below

My book on Windows 11 Operating System

Another area I covered in the chapter 1 of this book is computer terminology. These are the major terms you need to know for easy understanding of this book. I will be using some of these terms frequently as we make progress.

The last part of chapter 1 was on how to setup a new Windows Operating System computers. This concerns those that are yet to buy their own computers. I was able to detail everything out in a way that someone that have not used computer before now will follow up. It was accompanied with few Illustrations to make the task easy to complete. So, we are in this chapter for continuation of the learning.

Mastering Your Computer Keyboard
Keyboard is one of the major parts of a computer that users always interact with. As a user of a computer, you must always use keyboard to type texts. This is the reason I want to explain keyboard so that you will not find it difficult anytime I say you should type something in your computer. If you can make use of the keyboard of your smartphone, you can also make use of the keyboard of the computer you are using because both are modelled almost the same way.

But for clarity because this book is created for beginners and seniors in different countries, I will guide you on some important keys. Understanding these keys will help make you a better user of computer machines.

The photo of a modern computer keyboard

The above photo is that of a keyboard. But know that the configuration of some keyboards may vary, but all of them look alike at the end. There are alphabet keys which are from A to Z. So, if you want to type some texts, you keep punching the keys until you are done with what you are typing.

The alphabet keys of a computer keyboard

In addition, there are 26 alphabet keys in a computer. The above photo is the way the alphabet keys are arranged on a keyboard.

Another key set that is on the keyboard are number keys. These are the keys you are to press if you want to type any number on your computer.

The number keys of a computer keyboard

The number keys are the first set of keys on the computer keyboard. When you want to type some numbers on any app of your computer or during naming of any file or folder, the number keys are the ones you are to press. If for instance I want to type two thousand in figure, all I need to do is to press key "2" and "0" three good times. That is all.

Other keys that are on your computer keyboard are the special character keys. As the names of these keys sound, they are special indeed. These keys are usually attached to other main keys like number keys. The photo below indicates the special character keys.

The Special character keys of a keyboard

If you want to press some special character keys, you need to press a key before you press the key that they are attached to. Let me make it practical. If you want to type @ key for instance in a Microsoft Word, press and hold the **Ctrl** key of your computer keyboard and then press key **2** (but this is dependent on where the special character is positioned on your keyboard). This will make the @ special character to be typed in the Word document. Use the same approach to type keys like #, $, %, & and others.

There is another key on a computer keyboard called the **Spacebar** key. This key works the way its name sounds. It is used to create space between words. If for instance I want to type the words "**Go home**" on Microsoft Word document, when I type **Go**, I must press the Spacebar key for it to create space before I type the second word **home**.

*The **Spacebar** key of a computer keyboard indicated*

As you can see in the above photo, the spacebar key is the longest key on a computer keyboard. Use it to create space where needed as you type some information using the keyboard.

The Caps Lock key is another key of a computer keyboard that you need to know. With this key, you can enable text capitalization before you start typing the text.

The Caps Lock key indicated

Take for instance I want to type the words "excellent book" in capital letters, all I need to do is to press the **Caps Lock key** before I start the typing of the words. Sometimes, once you press the Caps Lock key, a blue light shows on one part of your computer keyboard, but this depends on the way the keyboard was designed by the manufacturer.

Another key that is on the computer keyboard is the **Enter** key. You can use it to introduce new paragraph in your document. Let me assume I am typing letter in a document and at a point needs to introduce a paragraph, all I need is to press the **Enter** key. On doing that, I will jump to the next line and then continue with my typing.

The Enter key of a keyboard indicated

Another thing you can use Enter key to do is to save some text you have already typed on certain parts of a document. Let me break it down more. If for instance I want to rename a folder, after typing the name of the folder, I will hit the **Enter** key for the new name I typed to be saved.

Arrow keys are among the important keys on the keyboard. With the arrow keys, you can move the cursor on the screen of your computer to different directions.

The arrow keys of the keyboard

Take for instance I am typing in Microsoft Word App, and at I point I discovered I made a mistake somewhere on the document, I can use the arrow key to move my cursor to that part of the document and get the mistake corrected. There are four arrow keys on the keyboard. The keys point left, right, up and down. Just use the keys to navigate to different parts of any opened app where it works.

Another important key you need to know about is the **Backspace** key. The Backspace key is used to move the cursor back.

*The **Backspace** key indicated*

It can also be used to delete some letters you already typed. When you press the Backspace key, it moves the cursor back and delete any content/letters in that direction. It is the key I interact with frequently anytime I am working in Microsoft Word app. The number of times the Backspace key deletes texts depends on the number of times you press it.

The **Delete** key is another key on the computer keyboard. This key does almost the same job of the Backspace key.

*The **Delete** key of the keyboard*

When you press the Delete key of the keyboard, it deletes the words close to the cursor in the left direction. You can also use this key to delete images from any app, an example Microsoft Word or PowerPoint. To complete the task, just select the image by just clicking or tapping on it once. The next step is for you to press the **Delete** key. Immediately you do that, the selected image is deleted.

Modifier keys are the other keys you will see on a computer keyboard. The name Modifier is a group name. It comprises group of keys. Modifier keys are the **Windows logo** key, **Alt** key, **Ctrl** key and the **Shift** key. They are individual keys but are grouped under that name.

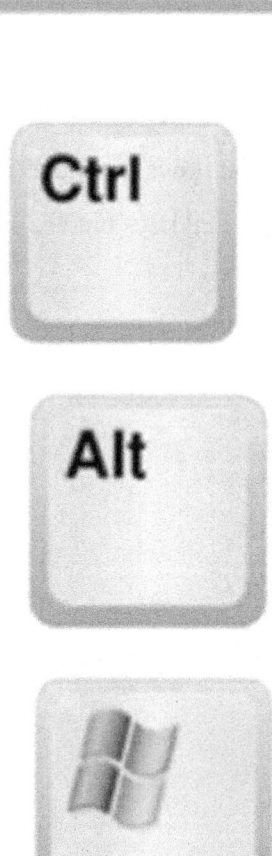

The photo of the Modifier keys of a keyboard

If you click the **Windows** key of your computer keyboard, it will open the **Start** menu of your computer. You can combine the Windows logo key with the other keys of your keyboard to complete a particular task just like the other modifier keys. That is the reason they are called modifier keys. The Control key (Ctrl) can be used in combination with other keys as shortcuts for menu commands. Also, the Alt (Alternate key) can combine with other keys of your keyboard to work as shortcut for menu commands.

The **Function** keys of the computer keyboard comes after the Esc key. The photo below indicates the function keys of the computer keyboard.

The Function keys of a keyboard indicated

With the function keys, your computer can perform certain functions. They are named from F1 to F12 at the top of the keyboard section.

Though as I writer I do not use Tab key frequently, it is one of the keys of a keyboard you may like to know.

*The **Tab** key of a keyboard indicated*

With the **Tab** key, you can move the cursor of your computer to the next tab stop. It works in a way that it pushes the cursor towards the right, and you can continue your typing from there if that is what you want.

As a beginner in the use of computer years back, I did not thoroughly understand the importance or usefulness of a key of the keyboard named **Esc** key (Escape key).

The Esc key of a computer keyboard indicated

With the Escape key, you can cancel the operation you previously performed on your computer. Take for instance I copied a document on my computer, I can press the Esc key for the copy I made previously to be cancelled.

Connecting Your PC to the Internet
Internet is an important network that connects computers from different parts of the world. Computers as used in this context includes smartphones. But that is by the way so that we can face what we are here for. When you are connected to the internet, you can access tones of information. Without internet connection, you won't have been able to view this my book, before buying it from Amazon global marketplace or its expanded distribution channels.

Some people know how to connect to internet on their smartphones only. They find it difficult on how to make their computers have internet access. As this book is for beginners and seniors who want to learn some things about the internet, I will walk you through on how to get your computer connected to the internet and on how to browse the internet using internet browser installed on your computer.

How to Connect Your Computer to the Internet Using Wi-Fi
One of the ways you can connect your computer to the internet is through Wireless Fidelity (Wi-Fi). According to network experts, the use of Wireless Fidelity provides internet to some machines, examples computers and phones, using radio wave which is of high speed. In a nutshell, you can connect that your computer to the internet via Wi-Fi method. When this happens, the internet of another device, example router, is shared to your own computer. It is like someone allowing you to share part of his room for a certain period of time. So, he gives you that opportunity.

Turn on the hotspot of the internet source. This can be hotspot of a router or the hotspot of your phone that has internet subscription in it.

To connect your computer to the internet through Wi-Fi, go to the Quick Action Center of your computer and then click the **Wi-Fi icon** just as you can see in the photo below.

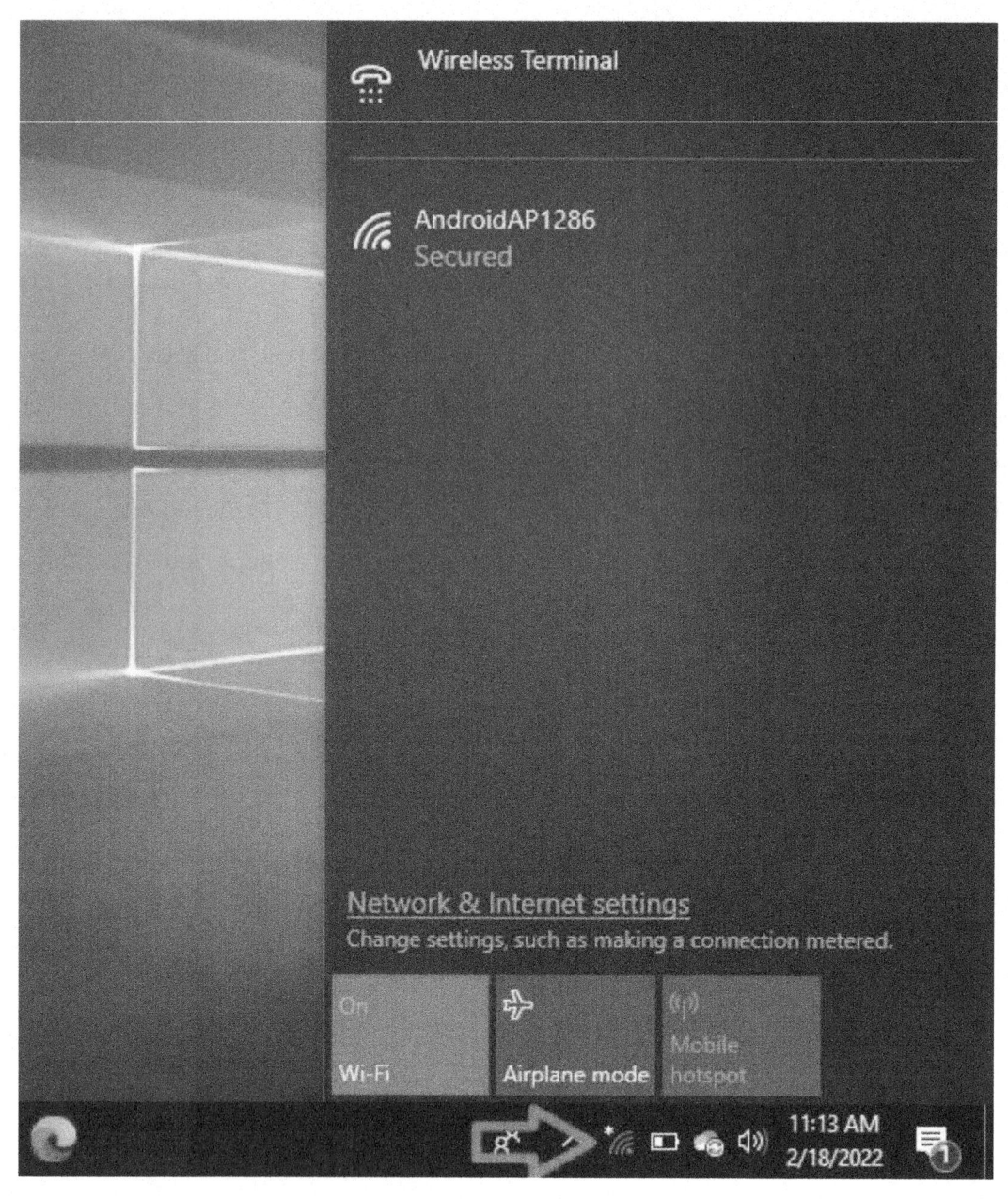

The Wi-Fi icon at Quick Action Center of Windows 10 computer indicated

As the Wi-Fi icon is clicked, it displays the hotspots of different devices that are turned on. But from the above photo, only one device hotspot is turned on. Click on that hotspot you want to connect to. Referring to the above photo, the hotspot I want to connect to has its name as **Android1286**. So, I am to click on it. As the click is made, you will see similar thing like the one I have in the photo below.

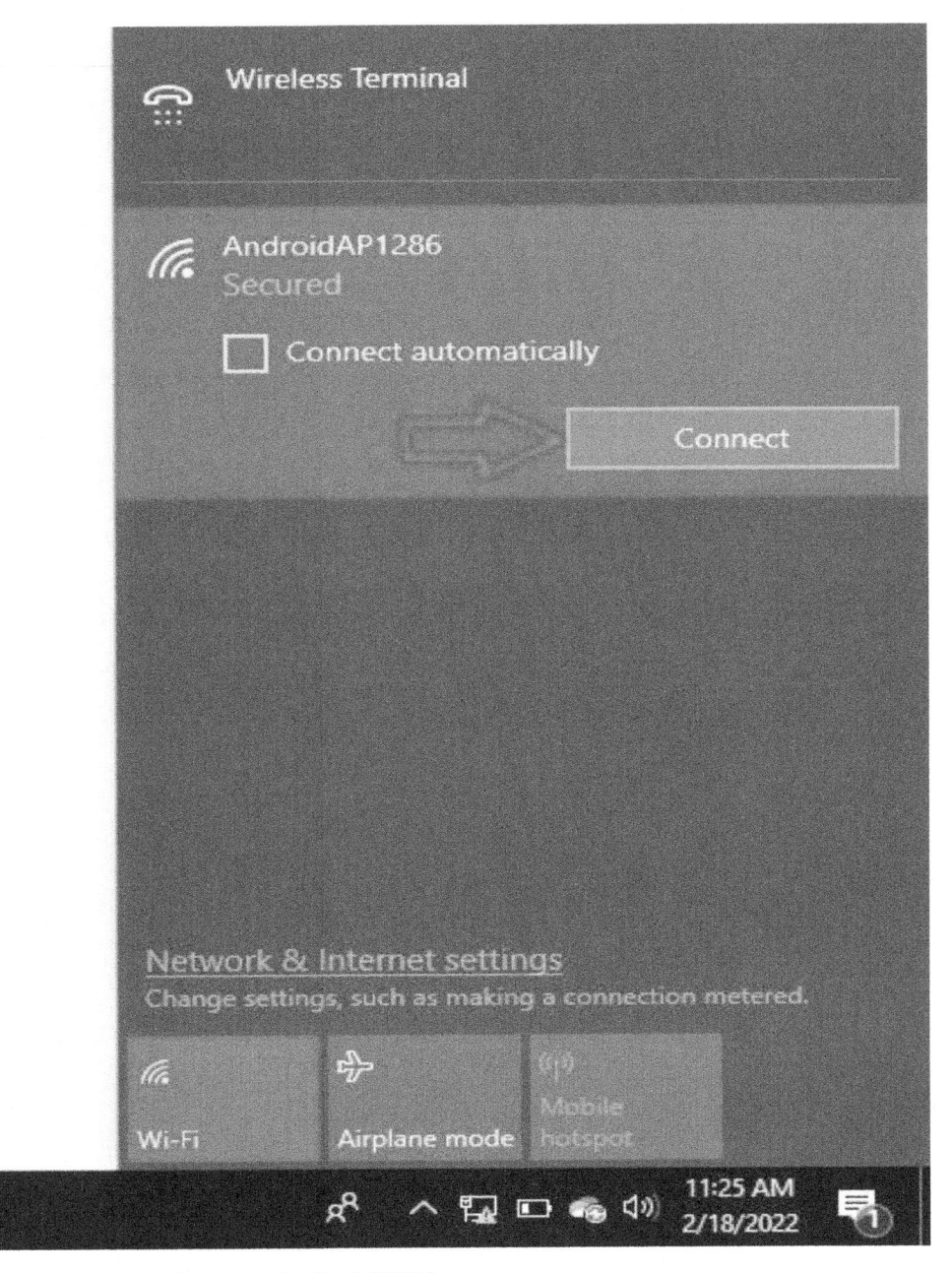

*About to connect to hotspot **Android1286***

The next step you are to take is to click the **Connect** button which I indicated in the photo above. You may be required to enter password of the hotspot from which you want to tap internet data from. If that is required, just type it and then hit the Connect button again. Once the system confirms that the password you entered is correct, your computer will be connected to the internet using the mobile data from the hotspot device.

I want to bring something to your notice. If you observe, when I clicked the hotspot I wanted to connect to, there is a box with the text **Connect automatically.** You can tick that box if you want your computer to connect automatically to the hotspot you are connecting to anytime it is turned on.

Connecting Your Computer to Internet Through USB Tethering
Another way you can give internet network to your computer is via the option called USB tethering. I am exploring options to give internet access to your computer because I will be using internet connection to complete some tasks in a computer in some subheadings ahead. So, I do not want you to say you do not know how to give internet to your computer or say you do not know how to get you PC connected to the internet. So, learn it all.

With the USB tethering option, you can share that internet subscription you have in your phone with your computer so that you can easily surf the net through your computer. So, first of all, turn the mobile data of your phone on.

Where to tap to turn on the internet network of your phone indicated

From the above photo, the internet of the phone is already turned on. So, if yours is still off, turn it on.

The next step you are to take is to use suitable USB cable to connect your phone to your computer. Currently, my main phone is Samsung Galaxy S8+, the USB cable for the connection is what I display in the photo below.

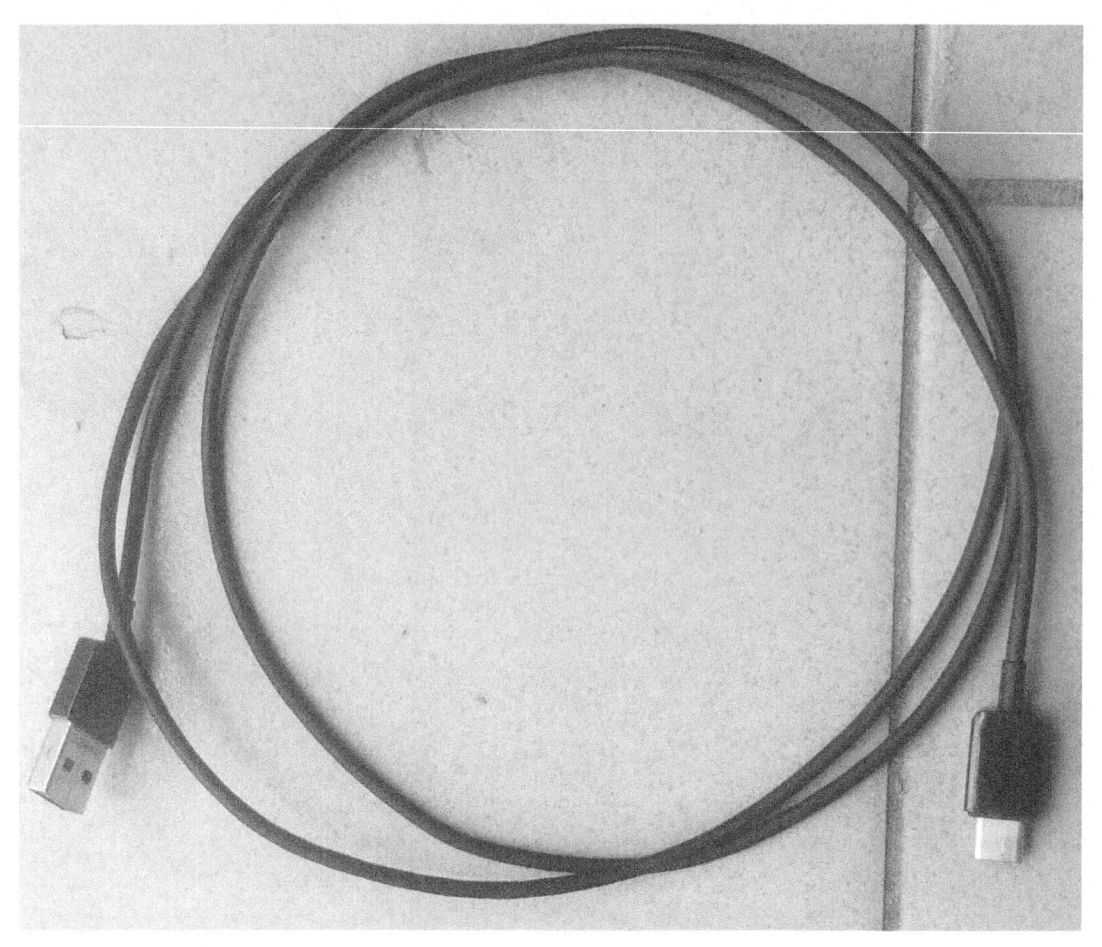

USB cable for smartphone to computer connection

In most situations, the USB cable should be the same cable you use in charging your smartphone. You do not need to stress yourself buying another USB cable.

Tap the **Gear icon** of your phone which is the phone **Settings**. The Gear icon representing Settings as one of the apps in my phone is displayed in the photo below.

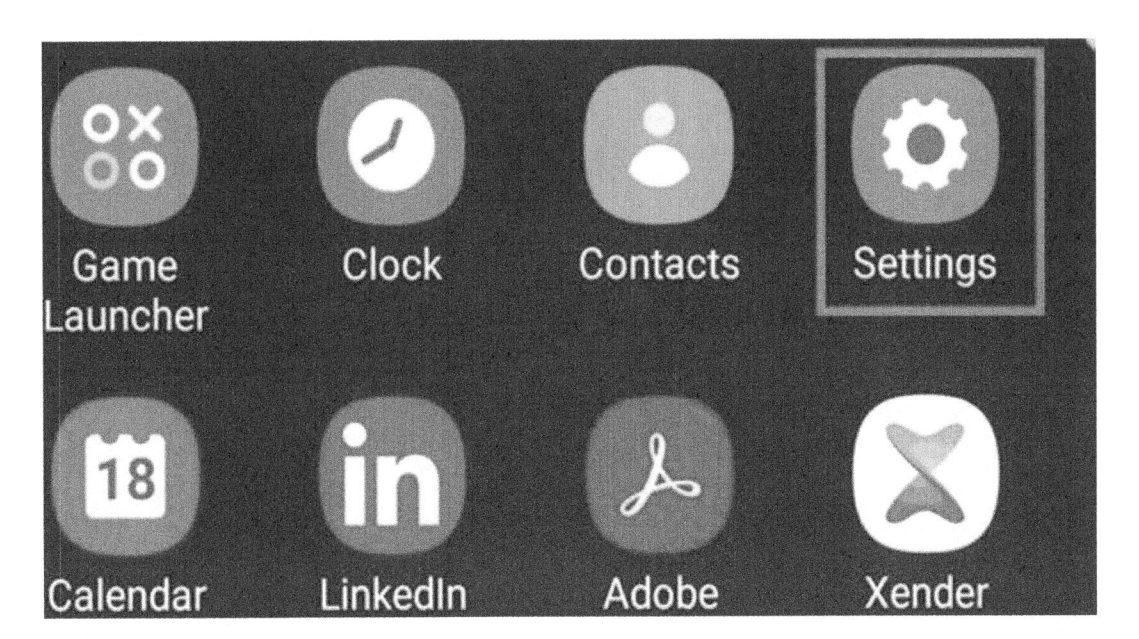

About to get to my phone Settings

As you click the Gear icon, the settings of your smartphone will be opened. Locate the **Connections** tab and tap on it (this may be modelled differently in different phones).

Settings

🔍 👤

Connections
Wi-Fi, Bluetooth, Data usage, Flight mode

🔊 **Sounds and vibration**
Sound mode, Ringtone, Volume

Notifications
Block, allow, prioritise

Tap the **Connections** *on the list*

As you tap **Connections**, a new page will open called the connections page. The page will look like the one displayed in the photo below.

42

NFC and payment
On

Flight mode
Turn off calling, messaging, and Mobile data.

Mobile networks

Data usage

SIM card manager

| Mobile Hotspot and Tethering |

More connection settings

The Connections page of Samsung Galaxy S8+

On that page, there are other sub-tabs, tap on **Mobile Hotspot and Tethering**. This action will open Mobile Hotspot and Tethering page. The page will look like what I have below.

*The **Mobile Hotspot and Tethering** page*

And lastly, the step you are to take is to toggle on the **USB tethering** button. As soon as you do that, the internet data of your phone will be shared with your computer. You can then browse the internet with your computer. Just browse any website of your choice from there.

How to Connect Your Computer to the Internet Using Modem
Since many computer users learned how to share the mobile internet data of their phones to their computers, the use of modem dropped. But for the purpose of this heading, I will teach you on how to do that. This is for you to explore all the available options for you to get the internet working on your computer.

Power your computer on. Slut in the USB modem to the USB port of your computer.

A modem plugged into the USB port of my computer

If the modem is being used in your computer for the first time, your computer will ask you if you want the device software to make changes to your computer, just agree with that. The modem drivers will install in your computer. Follow up with all prompts to complete the installation process.

Once the installation is complete, a new modem interface will show up on your computer screen. Just click the **Connect** button for the modem to connect your computer to the internet. At that point, you can start browsing the internet on your computer using any web browser. I will guide you in detail on how you can browse the internet using a web browser in a chapter ahead.

The Desktop of a Windows Computer

As you finish the setup or upgrade to a new Windows version, the first part of your computer you will see is the part called the desktop. The photo below is the desktop section of a computer running Windows 11 Operating System.

The desktop of Windows 11 computer

Desktop is design with a beautiful background image just as you can see in the photo above. Explaining further, desktop is the screen of your computer which you will see once you power on your computer machine. It is the physical workspace of a computer and taskbar is situated at the bottom part of it.

There are many things you can do on the desktop of a computer. I would have taught you a lot on some tasks you can complete on the desktop of your computer, but I will just walk you through on few because this book is for beginners and seniors. If I go deep on it, you may get confused.

Creating Folders on the Desktop of a Computer
Folders are important in computer use. A folder is like a container created on a computer that can contain many files. Take for instance you have some files about your finance and other files that are about health. Instead of having these files scattered all over the desktop of your computer, you can create two folders on your computer.

One folder will contain files about your finance and the other will contain files that have to do with health. So, let me guide you on how you can create these files.

The first step you are to take is to right-click on the desktop of your computer. You will see some options that will be displayed. From those options, select **New** followed by **Folder**.

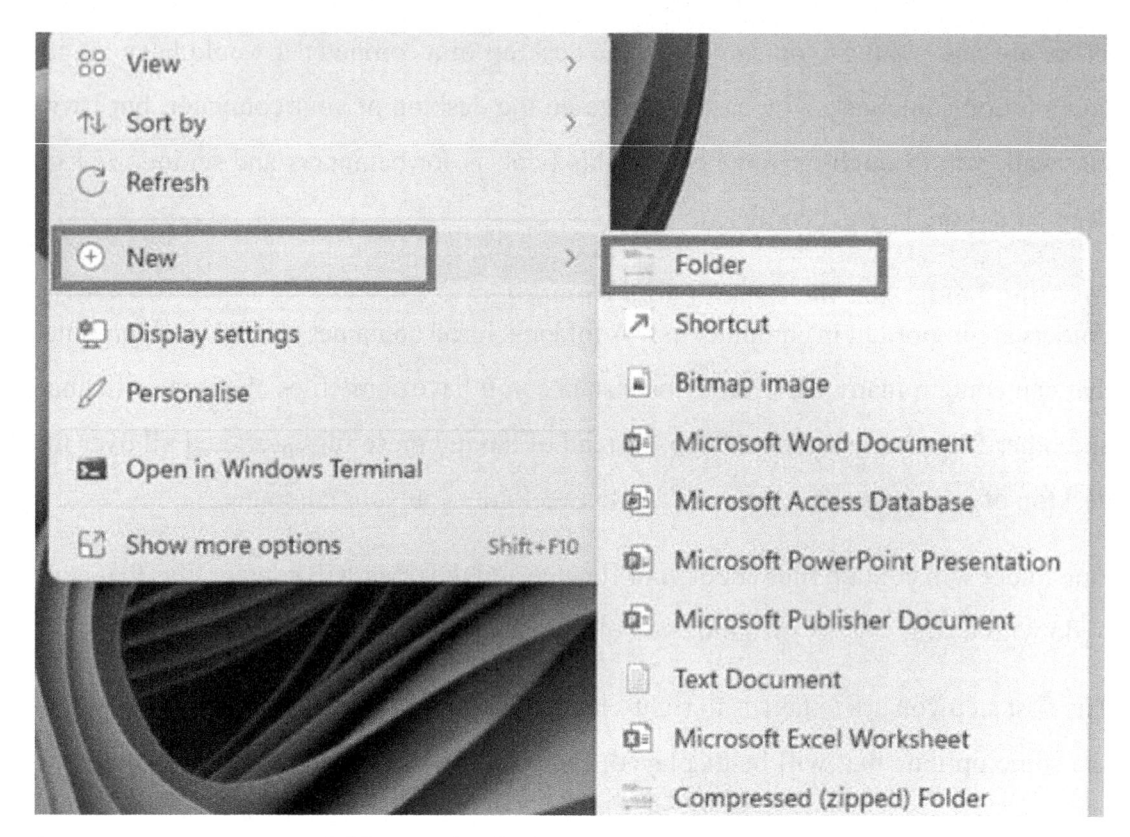

Progress in creating a folder on the desktop of a computer

A space will be provided for you to type the name you want the folder to bear. For example, you can type the name of the folder as **FINANCE**.

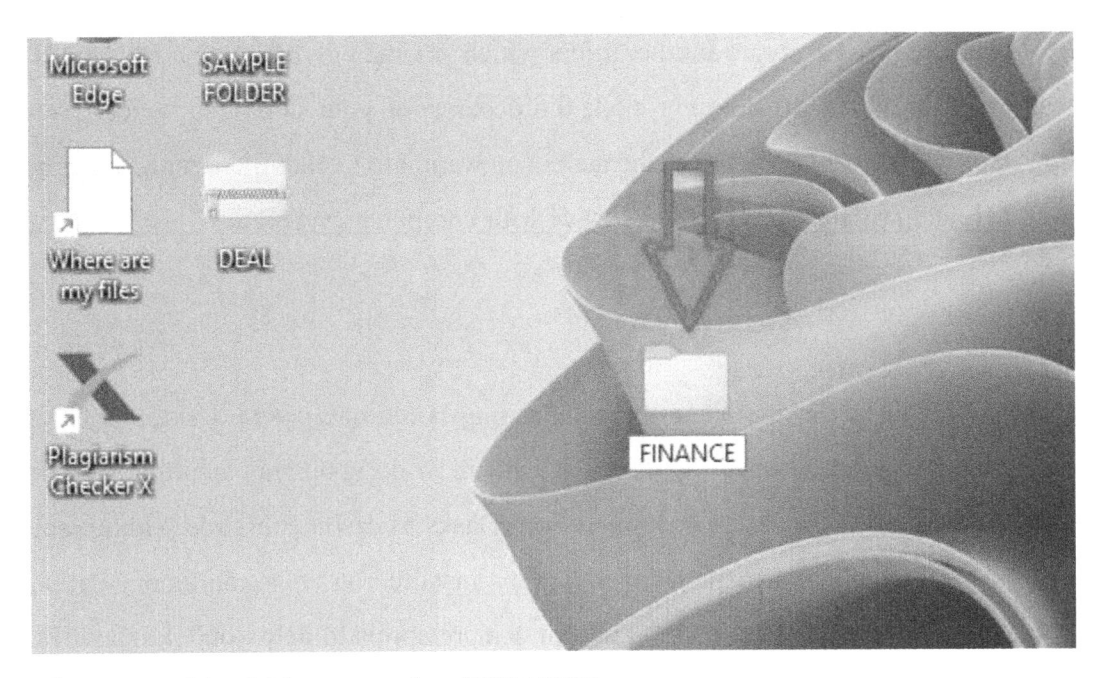

*The name of the folder entered as **FINANCE***

And lastly, press the **Enter** key of your computer keyboard for the name you typed to be saved. Incase you do not know where the **Enter** key of your computer keyboard is located, it is by the right-hand side. Also, the **Enter** key of a computer keyboard is indicated in the photo below.

*The **Enter** key of a keyboard indicated*

Once that Enter key is pressed, that new folder you created is saved with the name you gave to it.

So, follow these steps to create another folder which you may give the name **HEALTH**. In summary, the steps are to right-click the desktop of your computer, select **New** followed by **Folder**. Give the folder the name you want it to be identified with, example **HEALTH**, and lastly press the **Enter** key of your computer keyboard.

Working with Applications

The apps we will be discussing in this subheading is the one called desktop apps or computer apps. They are like the applications that are working on your smartphone. The reason for apps is to help you to complete some tasks as fast as possible without any stress. Take for instance, camera is an application installed on your smartphone before the phone is sold to you. The function of that camera app is to help you take pictures. So, some other apps have their specific tasks they help you to complete.

But, what is an app or application? A desktop application is program designed in a way that it can carryout a specific task in a computer. An example of an app is calculator app installed on a computer.

It is important you know about some apps that are preinstalled on your computer. Also, it is important you know how to install some apps you want to use on your computer. After the installation of some apps on your own, some of the apps may automatically appear on the desktop of your computer. This is for you to have easy access to the apps. There are many ways through which you can access some apps that are existing in your computer.

How to Access Apps Installed on Your Computer

As I stated earlier, there are ways through which you can access the apps installed on your computer and get them launched.

One of the ways is through the Search icon pinned at the taskbar of your computer. The photo below shows the Search icon I am talking about.

The Search icon pinned at the taskbar of a computer running Windows 11 OS

When you click the Search icon, type the name of the app you want to launch in the search space. The application will show up, and lastly click the app. When you click on the app, wait for few minutes and the app will be opened. This is one of the ways you can access and launch the apps that are installed on your Windows computer.

Another way through which you can access the apps that are installed on your computer is by first clicking the **Windows logo icon** of your computer.

*The **Windows logo icon** of a Windows 11 computer indicated*

As you click the Start logo icon (it is the same as the Windows logo icon), click the **All Apps** button at the right. The photo below shows the position of the **All Apps** button which you are to click.

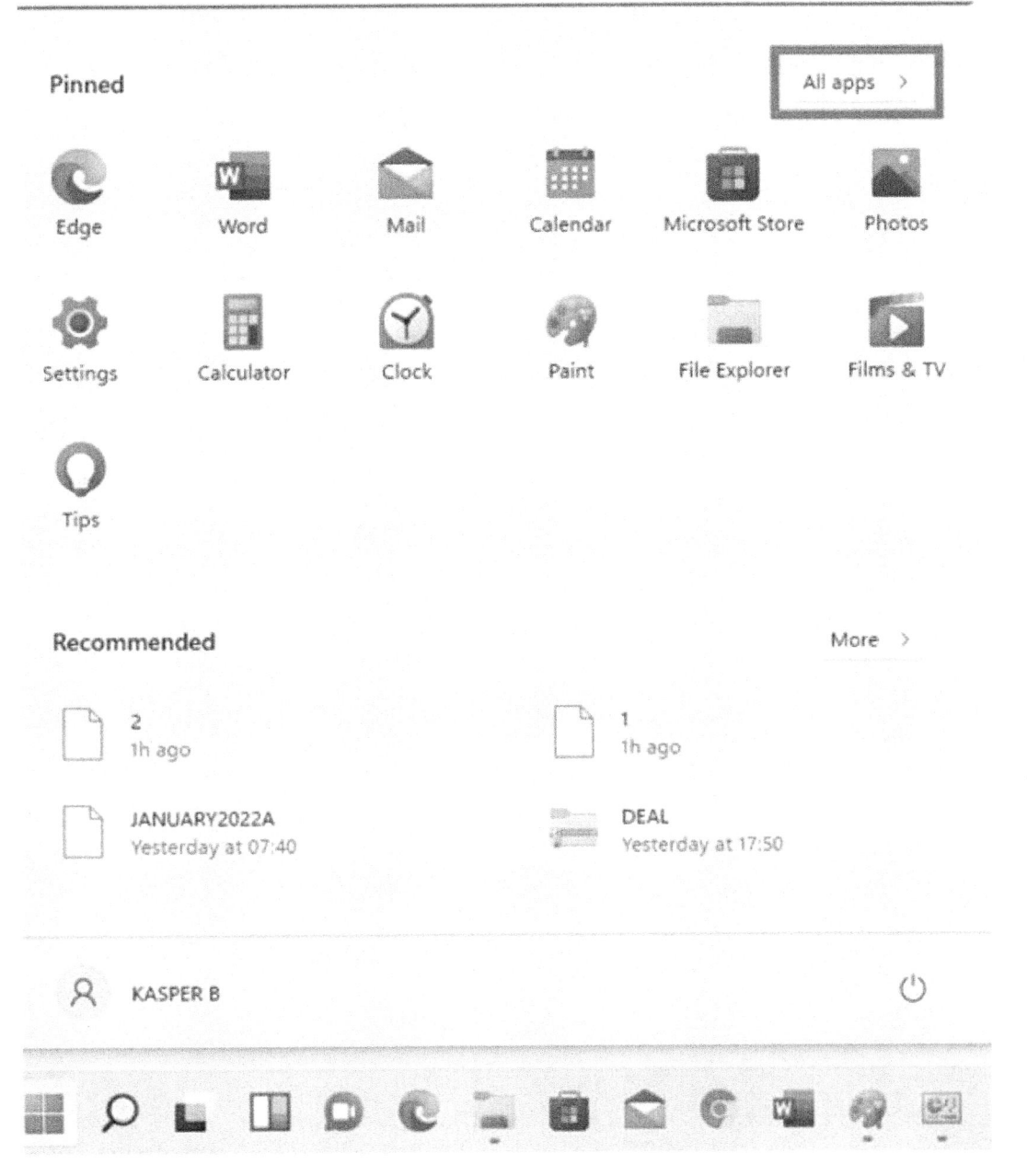

*The **All Apps** button indicated*

When you click the All Apps button, some apps that are installed on your computer will be displayed. You can scroll down the page to see as many apps as you want.

Another way you can view and launch few apps that are installed on your computer is through the Start menu of your computer. In this part of your computer, you will see some frequently accessed apps of your computer. To get to this section, just click the **Windows logo icon** of your computer. You will see some apps that are pinned at the Start menu of your computer which I indicate in the photo below.

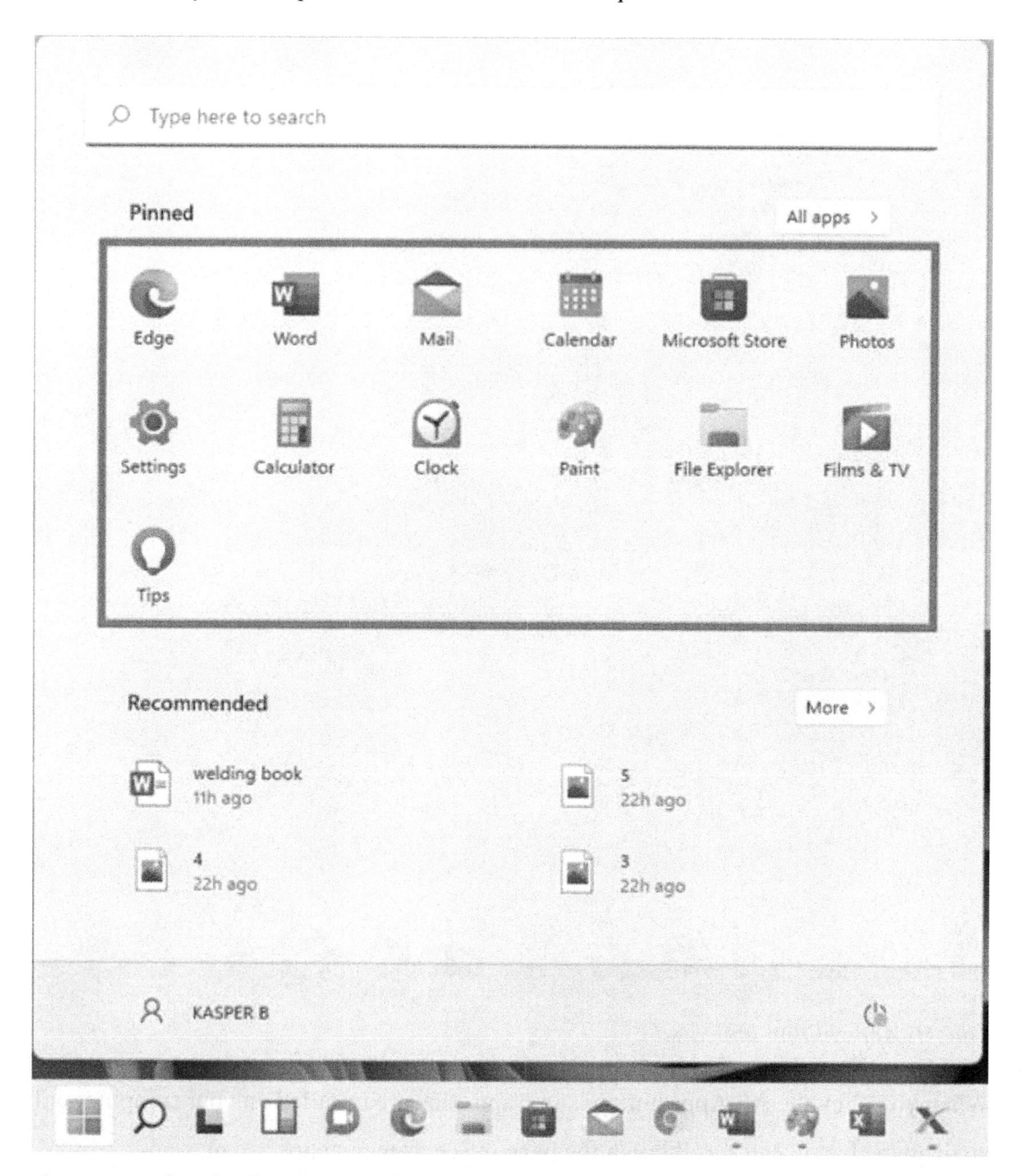

Apps pinned at the Start menu of my computer indicated

When you click on any of the apps, it will be launched, and you can start completing some tasks from there. From the above photo, the apps that appear at the Start menu are Edge, Word, Mail, Calendar, Microsoft Store, and others.

Getting New Apps in Your Computer

As a beginner or senior, there may be some applications you want to be interacting with most times in your computer, but they are not available in it. You may be wondering how to get those applications. They are all software, and you can get them up and running in your computer.

You may be working in a corporate organization and as a result of that needs few Office software to help you complete some tasks in the office. The two major most used Office software are Microsoft Word and Microsoft Excel. You can decide to go to a brick-and-mortar shop where these software are sold and get them installed on your computer.

The seller of the software will assist with the installation. If you have not heard about the word "install" or "installation" before now. To install a software means to put or setup an application on your computer in such a way that you can use it to perform specific task. Without installation of apps, there is no way applications can be useable in a computer.

On your own, you can get any app you want to use in your computer and then do the installation by yourself. Somebody must not help you to do it, and that is one of the reasons you bought this book. The reliable way to get an app and then install the application on your computer after getting it is through Microsoft Store app or Microsoft website. The photo below is the icon of Microsoft Store which is pinned at the taskbar of a computer running Windows 11 OS by default.

*The **Microsoft Store icon** at the taskbar of a computer*

If the app is not pinned at the taskbar of your computer, click the **Windows logo key**, and in the search space at the top, type the word "Microsoft Store". This action will bring up the Microsoft Store icon, click on it and it will open.

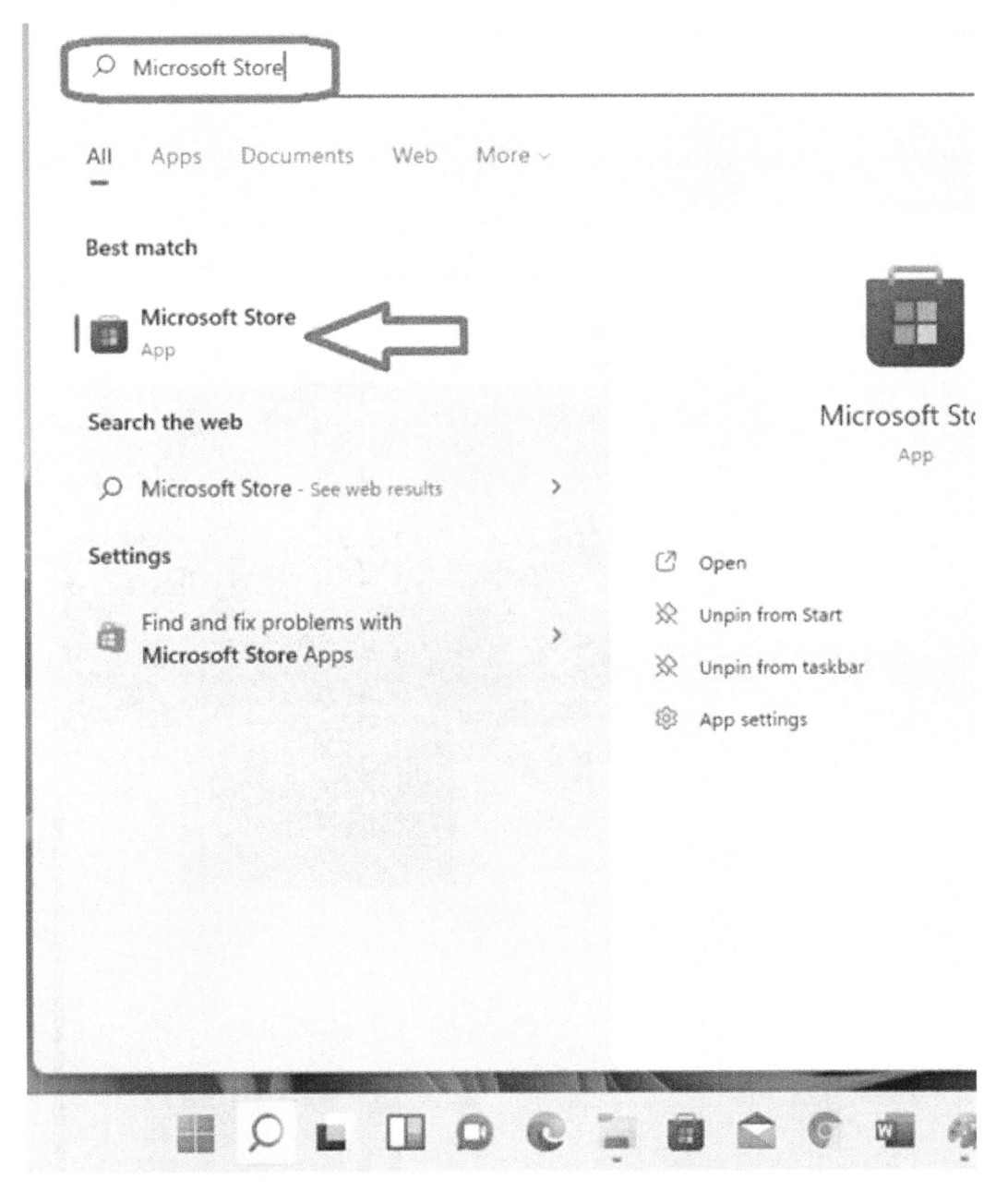

*About to launch **Microsoft Store app** through Search*

As indicated by the arrow in the above photo, just click the **Microsoft Store** for it to open if you want to access the Store via the Search of your computer.

Before you open the Microsoft Store, make sure your computer is connected to internet. This is because the store functions with internet connection. Microsoft Store is an app store owned by Microsoft, who are the developers of Windows Operating Systems. So, they created that store for users of their Operating System to be able to buy some apps as well as other services.

As the Microsoft Store app opens, you will see a platform that will look like the one I have in the photo below.

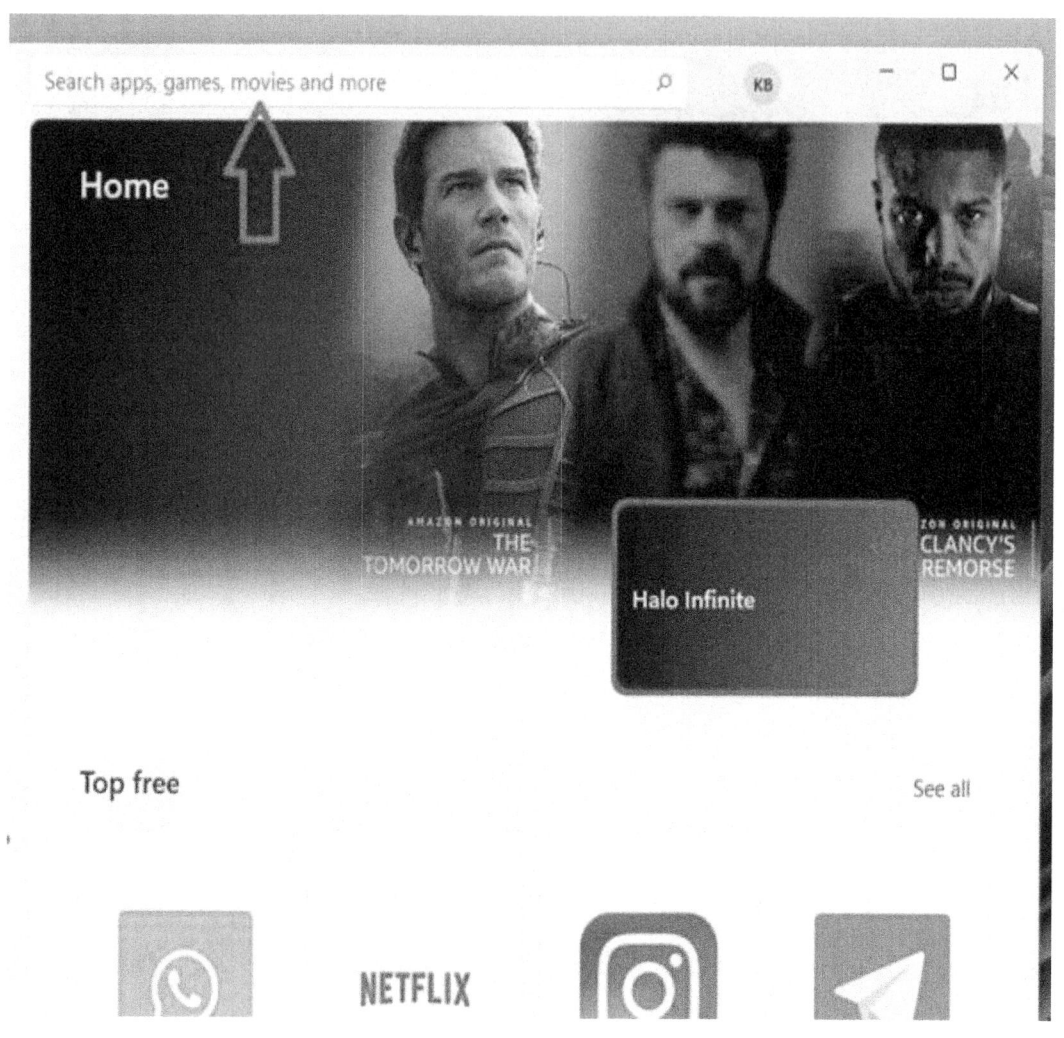

The Microsoft Store homepage

If you have not created account with Microsoft before accessing this store, Microsoft will advice you to do so. Without doing that, you cannot get anything from the online store. You can use your Gmail email address to create the account or even your you phone number, with password you will be using to sign in. If you have an existing account with Microsoft, and you are visiting Microsoft account for the first time, you will be required to sign in. Just follow the prompt and at the end you will be landed on the homepage of the Microsoft Store which I have in the photo above.

Do not forget that our interest is to Download and install the App we want to use in our computer to complete some tasks. Let me assume our interest is on Microsoft Word and Excel. So, in the search space indicated by an arrow in the above photo, type Microsoft Word. I think it will be good we start Word.

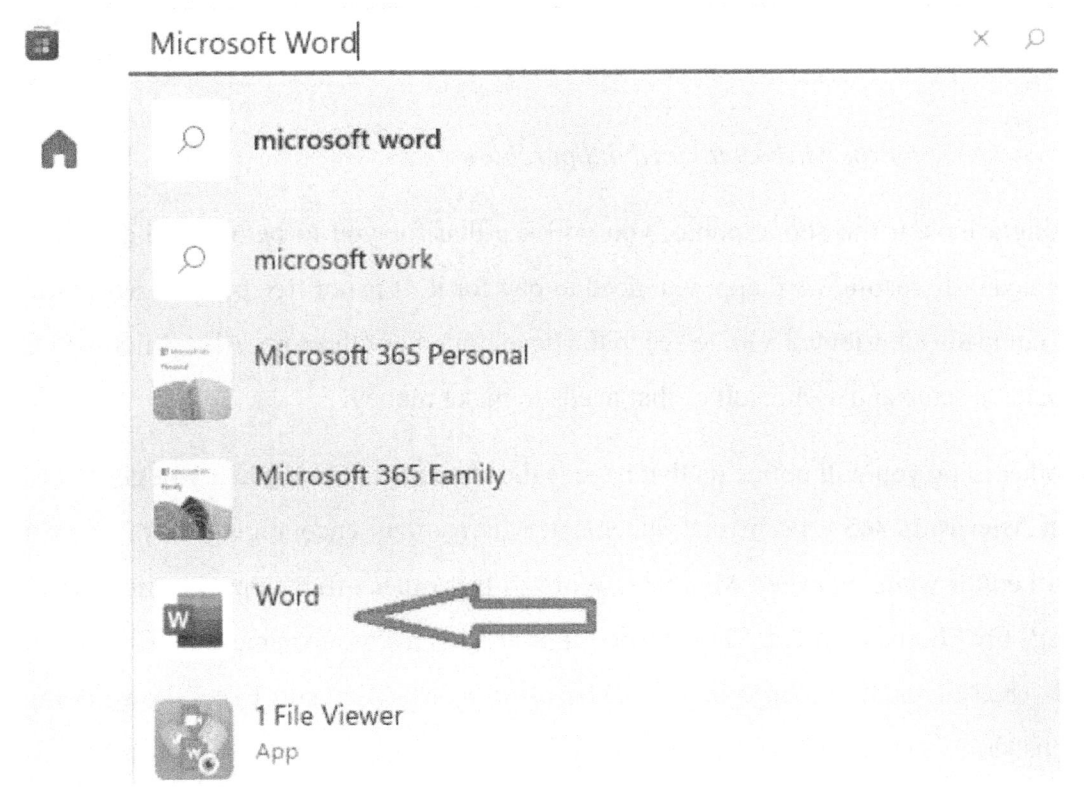

Microsoft Word app indicated by the arrow

Click on that **Word** App for it to open on a new page. What you will see will look like what I have in the photo below:

The new page for the Microsoft Word full purchase

Taking a look at the above photo, you will see that for you to be allowed access to download Microsoft Word app, you need to pay for it. It is not free because Microsoft as a company contributed a lot to see to the development of the App. Also, Microsoft is a business setup and as a result of that needs to make money.

Another thing you will notice on that page is the statement "**Save when you get Word with Microsoft 365**". From that statement, Microsoft is encouraging users of their Word editor which is called Microsoft Word to buy other office apps once instead of using only Microsoft Word. These Office apps are given a group name called Microsoft 365. The Microsoft 365 apps includes Microsoft Word, Microsoft Excel, PowerPoint, Publisher, OneDrive, Skype, and others. I recommend you go for that instead of just Word App because that is what I use currently in my computer. So, from the page shown above, pay to get it downloaded in your computer.

Making reference to the above photo, click the **For 1 person** which is positioned at the right-hand end of the photo. When you do this, a dialog box will show up asking you to choose a browser you want to use to open the purchase page. This is displayed in the photo below.

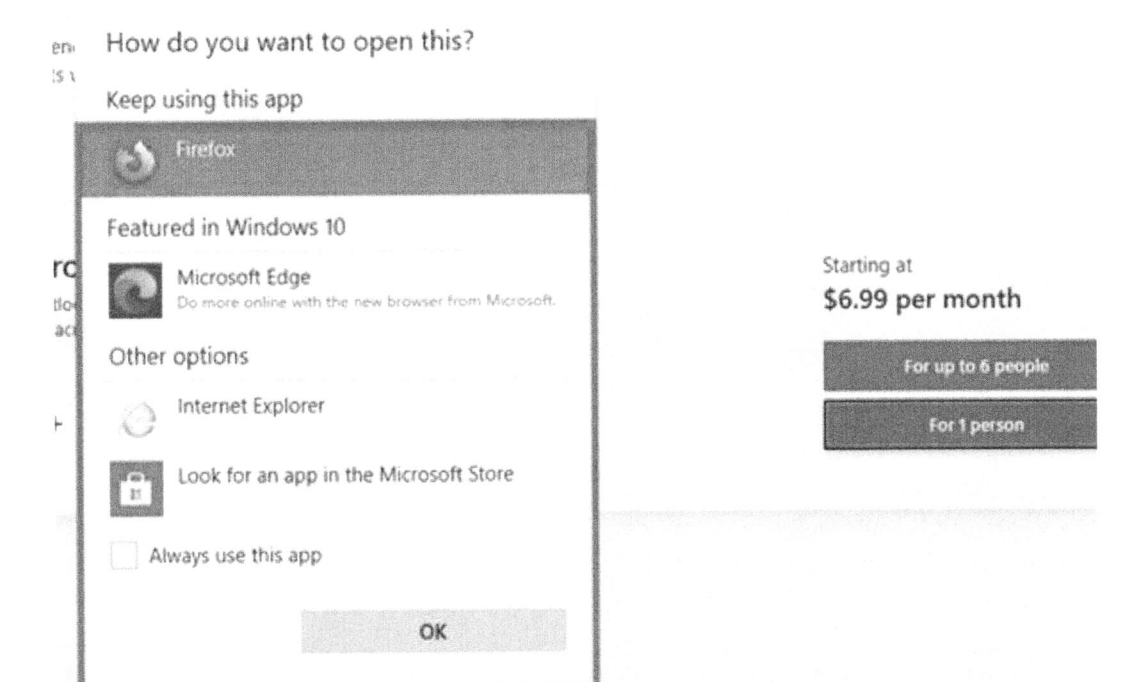

About to open purchase page for Microsoft 365 software

From the above photo, the browsers that are installed on my computer are listed. You can see Microsoft Edge, Firefox and others. So, if you see such on your computer screen, select any. But I recommend you select Microsoft Edge and then click the **OK** button. When you do that, a new page will be opened in the browser. There may be a popup requesting you type your email address followed by your country to signup for Microsoft out. If you have Microsoft account already, close that popup. On closing the popup, you will see a full purchase page. Scroll down the page until you get to the section I have in the photo below.

Microsoft 365 Personal — $69.99/year

Microsoft Corporation

For PC, Mac, iOS, and Android

One convenient subscription that includes devices.

With Microsoft 365 Personal you can:

- Access smart assistance features, plu PowerPoint
- Save and share files and photos acro
- Experience advanced security protec
- Use the subscription on up to 5 devi
- Contact support via chat or phone at

Buy and download

Or

Buy now $6.99/month

Need more users? Get Microsoft 365 Family for up to 6 people with 1 TB of cloud storage per person.

Subscription automatically renews. Cancel anytime to stop future charges*

About to continue with Microsoft 365 payment

Taking a look at the above photo, you can click on **Buy and download** for yearly subscription or **Buy now $6.99/month** to pay for just one month subscription. Anyone you can afford is okay.

On the next page, click **Checkout**. In the space provided for you to choose the payment method you want to pay with, I recommend you choose the option to pay with your bank credit or debit card. On completing your payment, the program will be downloaded in your computer.

The next step you are to take is to get to the Microsoft 365 downloaded program in your computer. By default, the file should be in the Downloads folder of your computer.

To get to the Downloads folder of your computer, click the **File Explorer** icon pinned at the taskbar of your computer for it to open, and then click on **Downloads**.

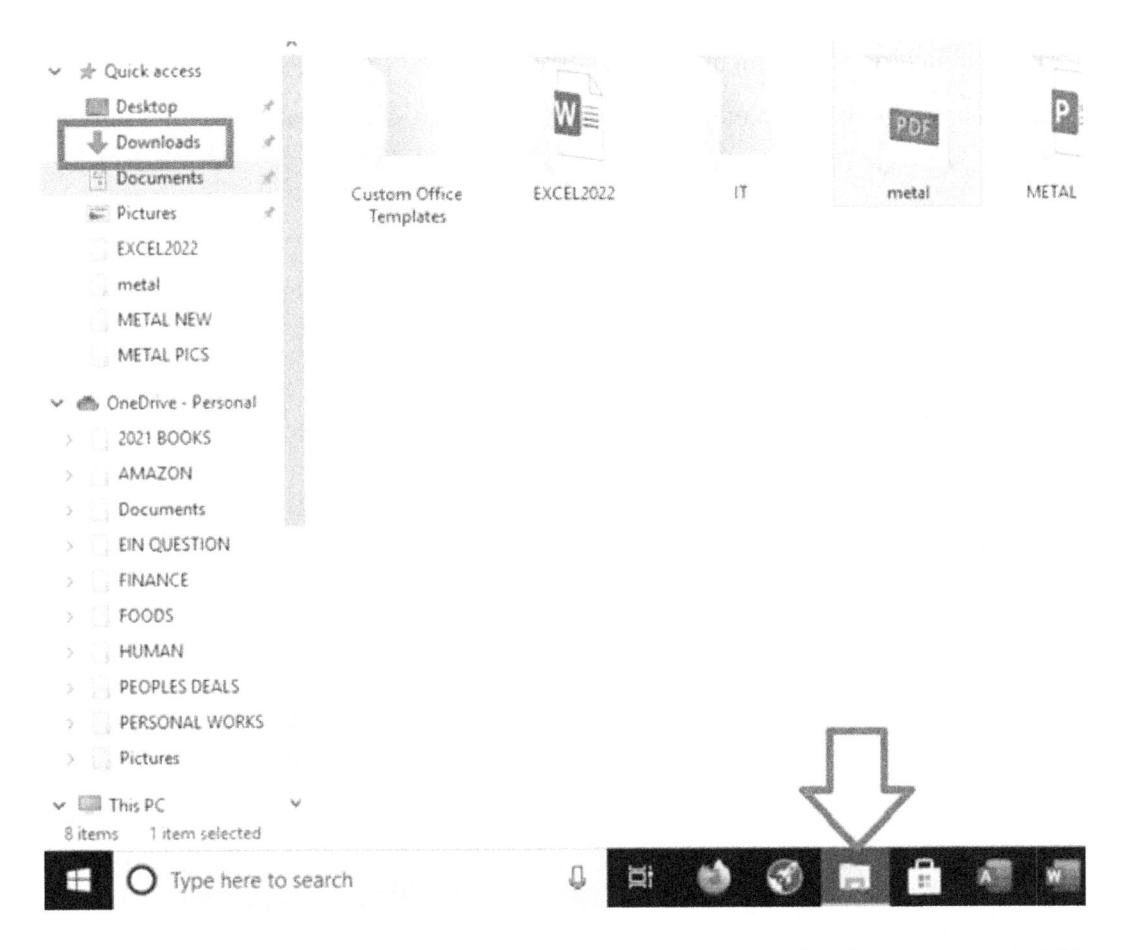

*The **File Explorer** icon pinned at the taskbar indicated, and by the **Downloads** folder*

When you click the **Downloads** folder, you will see some files that are downloaded from the internet into your computer. And one of them will be the Microsoft 365 program that we just downloaded. Double-click on that program. You will be asked whether you want the program to make changes on your computer, just accept. Follow up with the prompts, and it will take few minutes for the program to be installed on your computer. Once the installation is complete, click the **Windows logo key** of your computer, type the name of the app you want to launch, example Microsoft Word, and get it selected for it to open. At that point, you can start creating your documents with the app.

NOTE: Sometimes after downloading your Microsoft 365 software, the browser will prompt you to continue with the installation immediately. You will see words like **Setup**

or **Run**. Just click on any of them that pops up, and the software installation will begin. Once the installation is complete, you will see a notification on that.

CHAPTER 3

COMPLETING MORE TASKS IN COMPUTER

Welcome to a new chapter where you will learn something new about computer. This will impart a more concrete knowledge of computer into you and how you can perform some computer tasks on your own without relying on your grandchildren or a friend to teach you some things you can do on your own. It is another do it yourself chapter to make you a better user of Windows computers as a beginner or a senior.

In the just concluded chapter 2, I walked you through on the basics you need to know and learn in computer. I was able to guide you on how to launch apps. I did this with illustrations for you to understand every bit of the teaching.

In addition, I understood that many tasks you will come across in your computer will have your computer keyboard involved. As a result of that, I was able to explain keyboard to you in step by step. I pointed out some keys of a computer keyboard including alphabet keys, Backspace, shift key, delete, special character keys, Alt, Ctrl, Tab, Spacebar and other important keys of a computer keyboard. I put you through on what each of those keys can do for you.

I did not stop in the above, but I went further to talk about internet. I explained the term to you. In addition, I walked you through on how you can give your computer internet access. With clear photos, I covered how you can connect your computer to the internet via hotspot, USB tethering and through modem. I made all these explanations because I know the importance of internet connection to computers. There are some updates you can't make in your computer without first connecting your computer to the internet.

Other areas I covered in chapter 2 are the desktop of Windows computer, how to create folders on a desktop, and how to view some apps that are pinned at the Start menu of a computer. I did all these explanations with photos for your easy follow up with the teaching. Those teachings with easy step by step guide are continuing from here. So, learn with your computer fully opened and powered on in front of you. Let's move.

Apps at the Taskbar by Default
If you are making use of Windows computer recent versions, like Windows 10 or Windows 11, you will notice that at setting up your computer or installation of new Windows version, there are some app icons pinned at the taskbar section.

Windows 11 taskbar with different icons

Looking at the above photo, that section at the bottom with different icons is known as the taskbar. Some apps can be pinned at that part of your computer for easy access. When some apps are pinned at that part of your computer screen, once you give them a click, they become launched on your computer.

The first of the icons is called the Windows logo icon. The Windows logo icon is also called the Start icon, Start button or Start menu key. So, which ever one I use, I believe you should understand. When you click on the Start icon, you will see the Power button from which you can shut down your computer. I think I discussed this in chapter 1. In some older versions of Windows computer, the Windows logo icon is positioned at the left-hand side by default.

Another icon pinned at the taskbar of your computer by default is the Search icon.

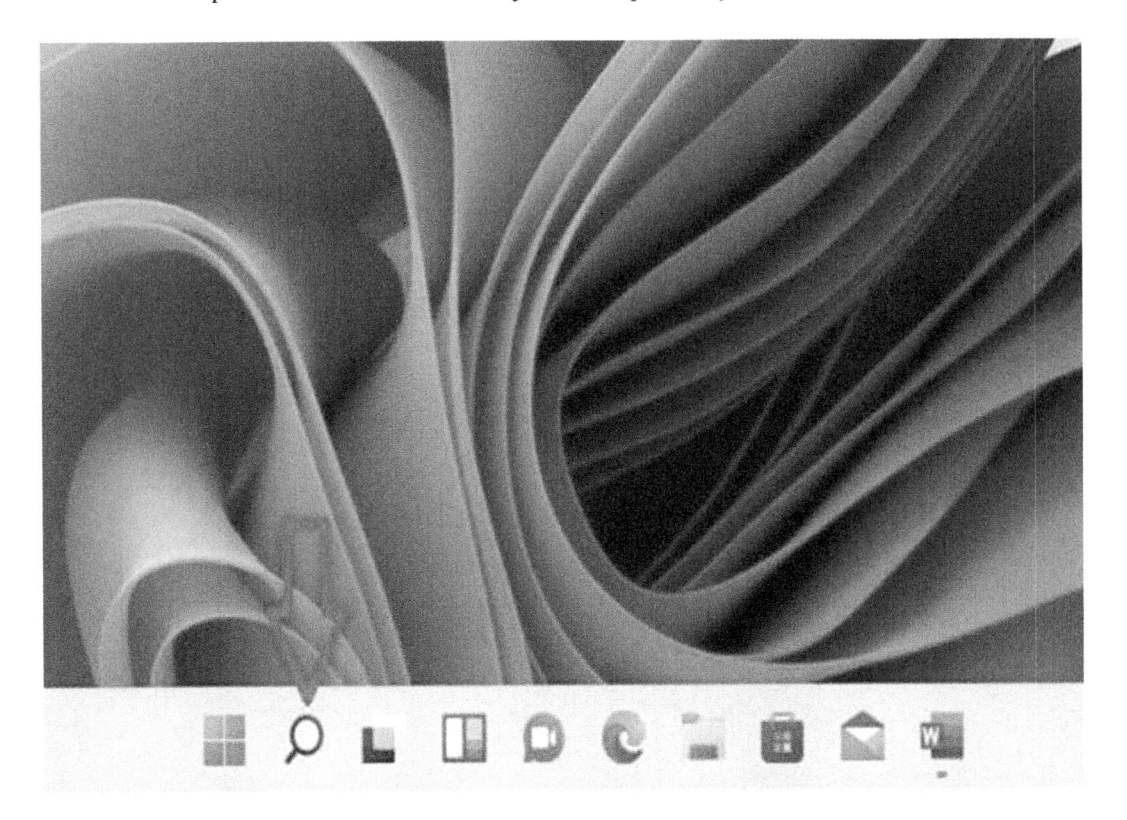

*The **Search icon** pointed by the arrow*

With the search icon, you can search through your computer or even the web. You can search for applications that are already installed on your computer and they will show up as one of the search results.

I have already taught you on how to install Microsoft 365 on your computer. This program contains major Office apps which you can think of, including Microsoft Word and Excel. Let me assume you installed it on your computer, and you want to create a document using Microsoft Word app. You can get to that app using the Search icon pinned at the taskbar, which from there can select the Word app to get it launched.

To achieve this, click that **Search icon** at the taskbar. This will open a search bar at the top of the screen. Type the text "Word" in the search space. This will bring up some search results relating to what you searched for. You can see that in the screenshot below.

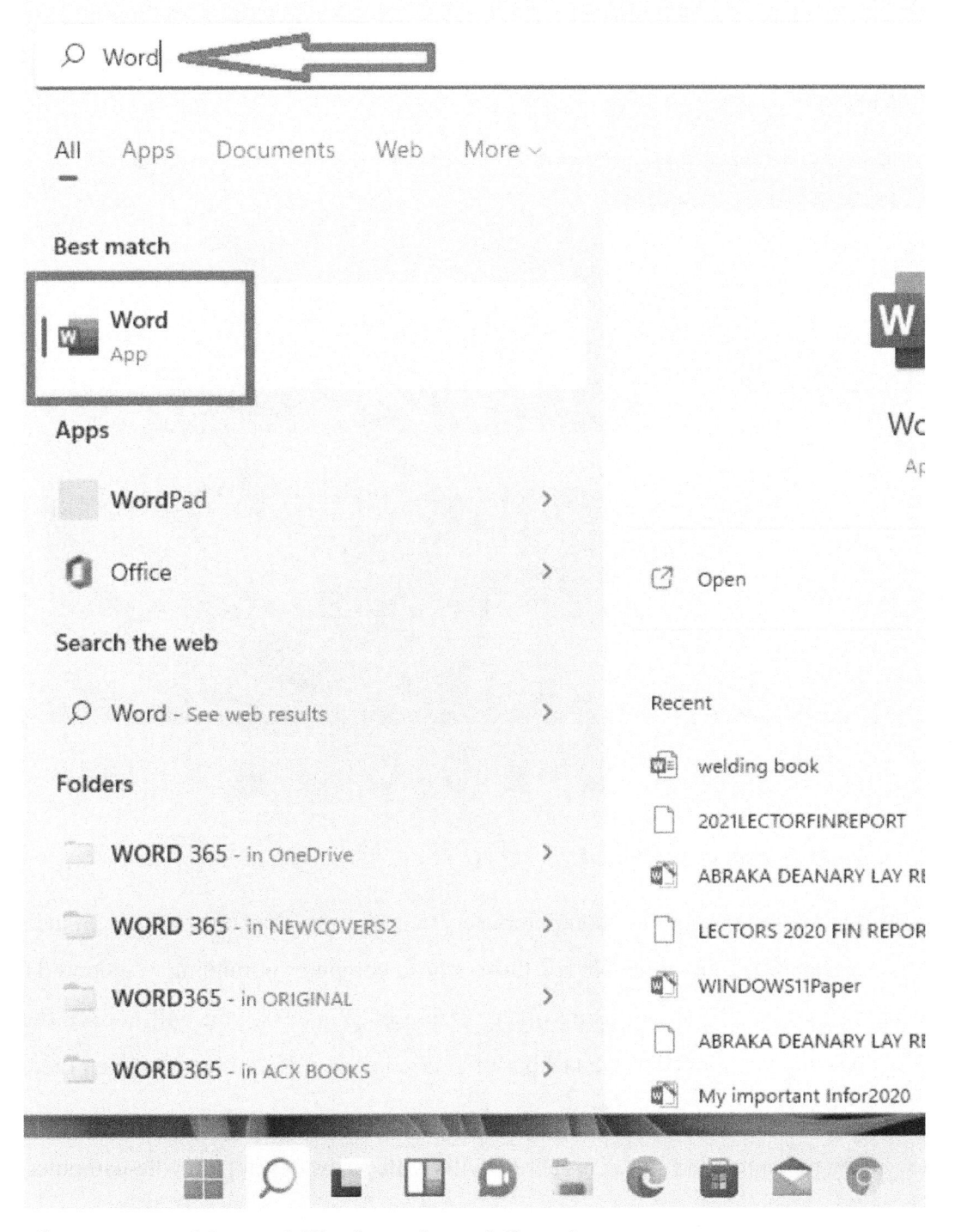

About to get to Microsoft Word app through Search app

As you can see in the above photo, the search result displays Word app among others, which I indicated in rectangle. Once you click on that app, it will be launched.

Another app that may be pinned at the taskbar of your computer after setting up your PC is the Virtual desktop app. The Virtual desktop icon at the taskbar is indicated in the photo below.

Virtual desktop icon at the taskbar

The Virtual desktop app allows computer users to open more than one desktop on their PC. This feature is only available for those whose computer is running Windows 11 Operating System. If you are using older version of Windows, you will not see the Virtual desktop app pinned at the taskbar of your computer. If you want to open more than one desktop, just click the **Virtual desktop** icon and then select the + sign that will show up by the right-hand side. This action will create a new desktop on your computer.

Widgets is another app pinned at the taskbar of most recent versions of Windows. Widgets is a utility functions app.

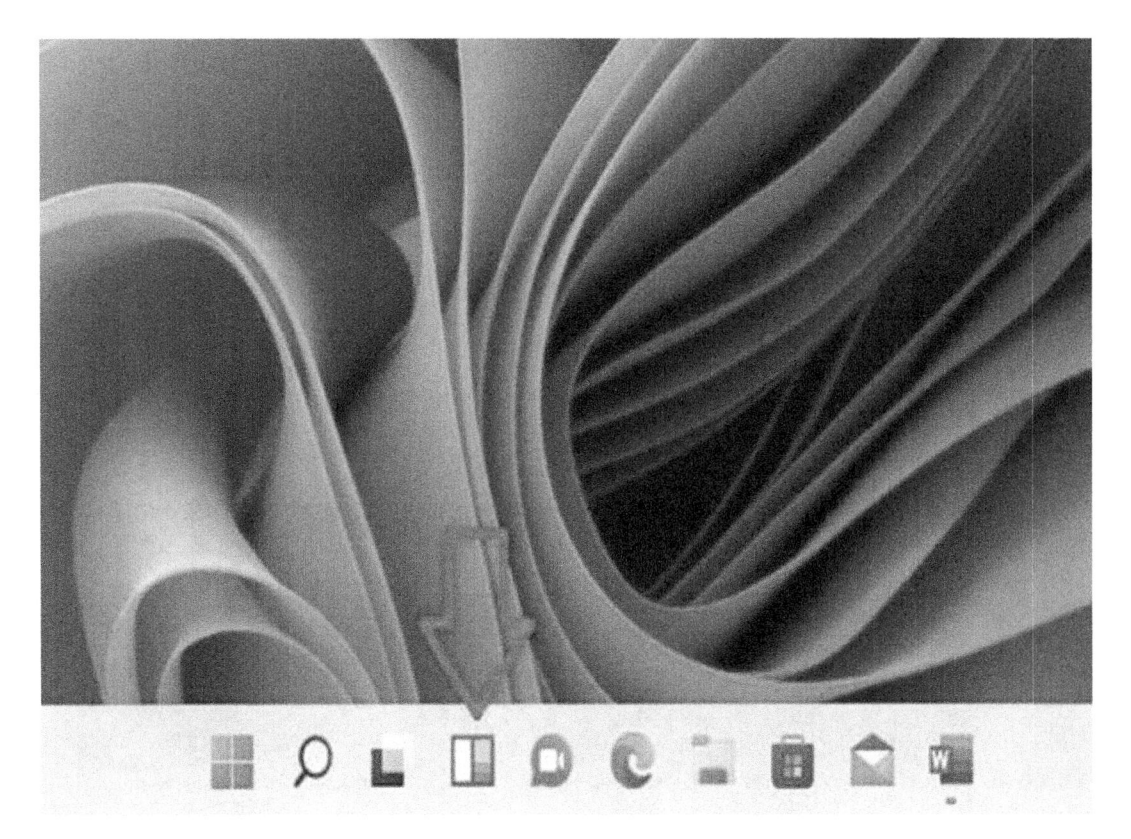

*The **Widgets app** indicated*

This app gives you notifications mainly on what is going on in your location and also on what you like browsing through the internet. When you click the Widgets app, it can display the weather of the day, news, and sports if you like browsing on sports using your computer. But know that for you to see any notifications using the Widgets app, your computer must be connected to the internet. I hope you have not forgot my teaching on how you can connect your computer to the internet.

Chat app is another app pinned at the taskbar of your computer by default if your PC is running the latest Windows Operating System. When you click the chat icon, you can set it up by following the prompt. At the end, you can use it to chat with your team. If you work in an office, many workers communicate with the chat app called Microsoft Team. It allows you to easily send messages to your colleagues, and they respond on viewing the message. It delivers fast and makes working with your coworkers easy.

Microsoft Edge is the latest Microsoft browser which works at high speed. It is built with many functionalities. In fact, with Microsoft Edge, you can pin some important webpages on your computer screen. It is a nice development be team of Microsoft software developers. Edge is a browser which you can use to browse the internet and it was developed by Microsoft. Microsoft is a multi-billion-dollar company pioneered by many times World richest man-Bill Gates. Edge is one of the apps pinned at the taskbar by default. I will teach you more on Microsoft Edge under "Using the Internet" subheading.

The Microsoft Edge app icon pinned at the taskbar of a computer

As pointed by an arrow in the above photo, you can click the Edge icon once for it to be launched. When it is opened, make sure your computer is connected to the internet for you to start browsing to different webpages. There is space where you can type the URL of a website, and you are taken there directly. On the other hand, there is a space for you to search anything on the web. In that space, you can type few texts and hit the search icon of the browser, and some search results will be displayed to you on your computer screen. Time will come when I explain that in detail with photos to ease your understanding.

There is no day I turn on my computer without interacting with the File Explorer. It does not happen. That is because it is a gateway to all the files that are existing in a computer. By default, Microsoft pinned the File Explorer to the taskbar because they understand its importance.

The File Explorer app at the taskbar of a PC

If I want to access some files that are not placed on the desktop of my computer, the first step I am to take it to click the **File Explorer** icon pinned at the taskbar. Once I do that, the app opens for me to locate the file I want to work on. The file can be document, video, pictures or any other file type. In fact, I do not like to save files on the desktop of my computer, so, I must click that File Explorer app to be taken to the part of my computer where I can navigate to the file I want to use.

Another app pinned at the taskbar of Windows OS by default is the Microsoft Store app. I Explained this in one of the early chapters of this book. When you click on the app, you will be allowed to download and install any application that will improve the functionality of your computer.

Mail is just a mailing app of Microsoft. That is another app pinned at taskbar of most recent Windows OS versions. The Mail icon as it is pinned at the taskbar is indicated in the photo below.

The Mail icon at the taskbar

If you have used Gmail or Yahoo Mail before now, the way they work is not different from the mail app pinned at the taskbar by default. The only thing you need to know is that the mail apps are owned by different companies. As a result of that, each of these companies want to promote their own products. They make money from them and that is the reason they do that.

The Mail app pinned at the taskbar of Windows Operating System is there because it is developed by Microsoft company. Because that is their own product, they want every user of their Operating System to make use of it. You can click that Mail icon, signup for it and then start making use of it to add to the one you may have with other companies like Google or Yahoo. But know that to signup for the Microsoft Mail is optional. It is a thing of choice. Most "big companies" make use of Microsoft Mail to communicate with their workers/team. So, it is a good mail servicing app.

Pinning Apps to the Taskbar

The reason why some apps are pinned to the taskbar of a computer is for easy access. When you do that, instead of getting to the app through the Search icon, you can just click on it once, and it gets opened. Also, instead of double clicking on an app when it is at the desktop of your computer, a click on the app when it is pinned to the taskbar will get it launched in short time.

In my computer, the apps I pinned at the taskbar on my own are those I use often to perform some tasks. These apps are Microsoft Word, Paint app and Plagiarism check app. I use the Word app to create my books, so it is a must pin app. The Paint app is what I use to create illustrations for my books, and it is needed to be there at the taskbar. And lastly, the Plagiarism app. I use the app to make sure that I pass plagiarism test on every book I write before the final publication. Can you see how important those apps are to me and the reason I pinned them to the taskbar?

You as an individual may have where you specialize on and as a result of that want to pin the app to the taskbar for easy access to the app. So, let me guide you on how you can pin an app to the taskbar of your computer screen.

The first step you are to take is to click the **Search icon** that is already pinned at the taskbar of the computer by default.

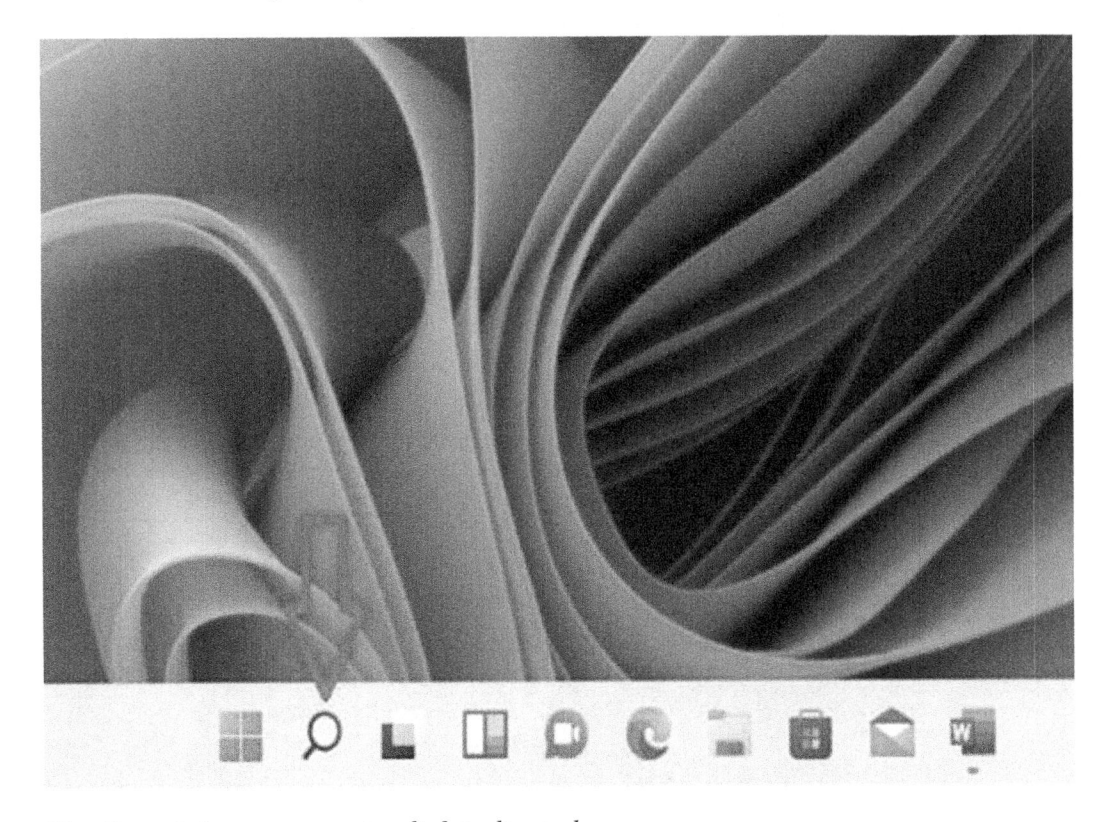

*The **Search icon** you are to click indicated*

As you click on the Search icon, a search bar will open for you to type the name of the app you want to pin to the taskbar section of your computer. An example is Excel which what I have in the illustration photo below.

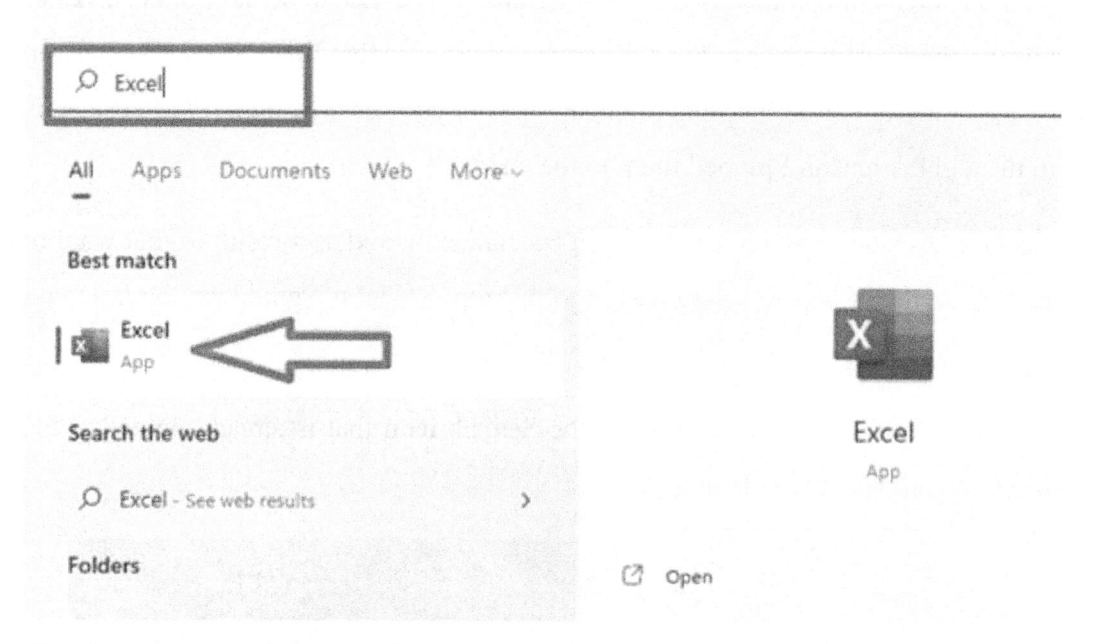

Excel app as one of the search results

When the app you want to pin at the taskbar shows up as one of the search results, the next step you are to take is to **right-click** on that app. On doing that, you will see some commands just like the one in the photo below.

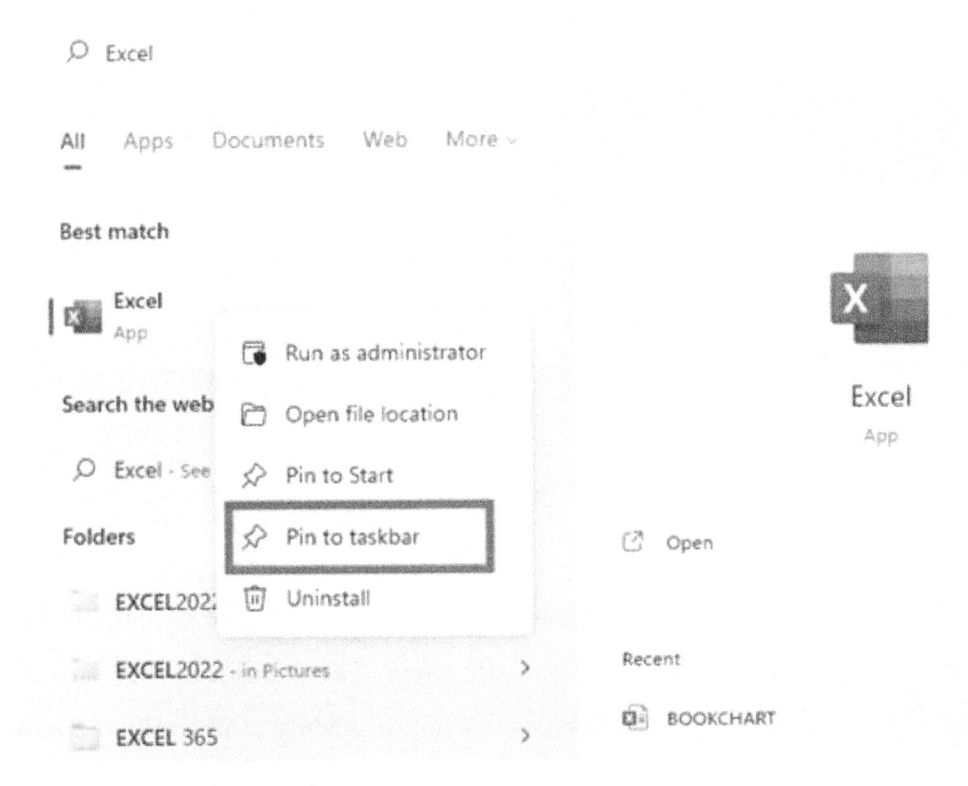

Right-click on the Excel app

And lastly, select the **Pin to taskbar** option by clicking on it once. Immediately you take this step, that app will be pinned to the taskbar of your computer screen. Follow this same step go pin as many apps as you want on the taskbar. But, know that it is recommended you pin apps that you use often in your computer.

The Basic Folders

As a beginner or senior, it is important you make use of folders to group your files. To access the basic folders of your computer, click the **File Explorer** icon pinned at the taskbar of your computer screen. As the File Explorer opens, you will see the basic folders made available on your computer by default. The photo below explains that.

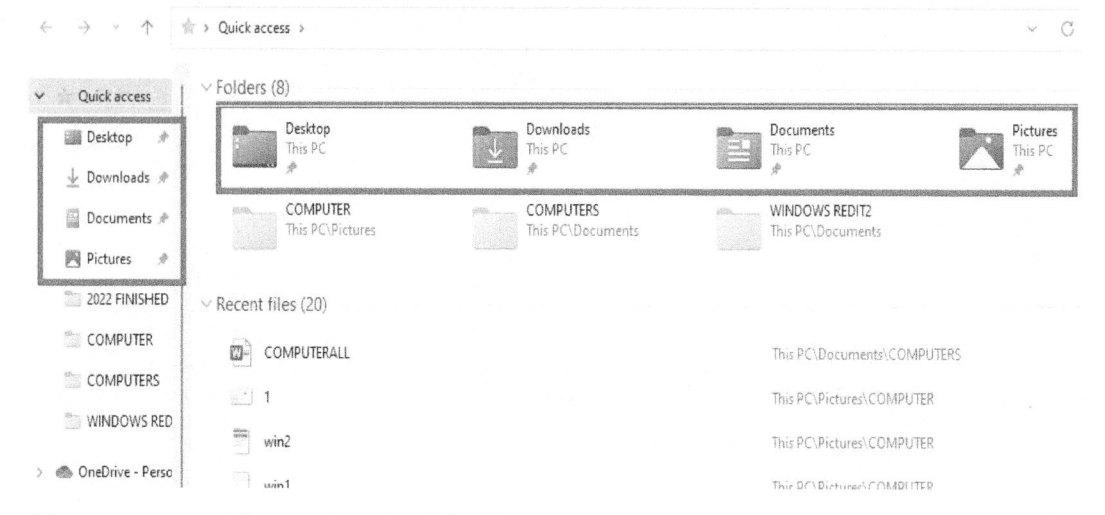

The page you will see when the File Explorer opens

Looking at the above photo, the major folders you will see when the File Explorer opens are Desktop, Downloads, Documents and Pictures. These folders are created automatically in your computer immediately on setup or when you upgrade to a new Operating System version. Inside these folders, you can create subfolders. Subfolders are folders created inside a main folder. I will explain that in detail under a new subheading.

Referring to the above photo, the first basic folder is named **Desktop**. I have explained desktop of a computer before. I stated that it that computer screen you see when you power on your computer. Any document, photo, or video you place in the Desktop folder will automatically appear on the screen of your computer. I do not like to paste documents I create on my PC in the Desktop folder, but you can do that if you like it. In addition, any apps you install on your computer in most cases are automatically placed on the Desktop folder. This is the reason you may see some apps you install on your computer appear on the screen of your computer as icons.

Downloads is the second folder you will see when you click on the File Explorer pinned at the taskbar of your computer. As the name sounds, this folder houses all the files you download from the internet browser into your computer. Take for instance I was searching for PDF document on a particular area of interest. If I download that document, it is automatically saved in the Downloads folder of my computer by default. The only exception is if I change where I want my downloads to be saved from the browser settings. Apart from that, the file gets saved in Downloads folder of my computer.

So, any time you are browsing through the web using an internet browser, examples Microsoft Edge, Mozilla Firefox and Google Chrome, once you download any file, click the **File Explorer** icon pinned at the taskbar, click the **Downloads** folder and you will see the file you just downloaded. Do not waste your time searching on other locations because you want to access the file you just downloaded from the web.

Another main folder you will see on clicking at the File Explorer is the **Documents** folder. This is created to contain all the documents you create in your computer. It is one of the major folders pinned at the Quick access. When you click the Documents folder as it is under the Quick access, it will open showing the documents in the folder. It is recommended you save the document files you create using any Word editor in that folder. Also, you can copy any document into that **Documents** folder.

Photos is the last in the list of the major folders you will see when you open the File Explorer of your computer. By default, the folder is to contain the images you like to have in your computer. If you just bought your computer and then set it up, you are likely to see some sample photos in the folder when you open it. That is to tell you that the folder was created mainly for saving of images. But that does not mean you cannot save other type of files inside it. You can have videos or documents files inside it.

How to Create Subfolders inside a Main Folder

As a writer, I save my written document files in Documents folder made available by default. But what if I write on software and business categories? Don't you think it will be fine to create two subfolders in my **Documents** folder where I will name one **SOFTWARE BOOKS** and the other **BUSINESS BOOKS**? That will be good as it will categorize the two types of books differently.

So, to create a subfolder inside the main folder, example **Documents** folder, these are the steps you need to take:

Step 1

Click the **File Explorer** icon pinned at the taskbar of your computer screen for it to open and display the main folders just as displayed in the photo below.

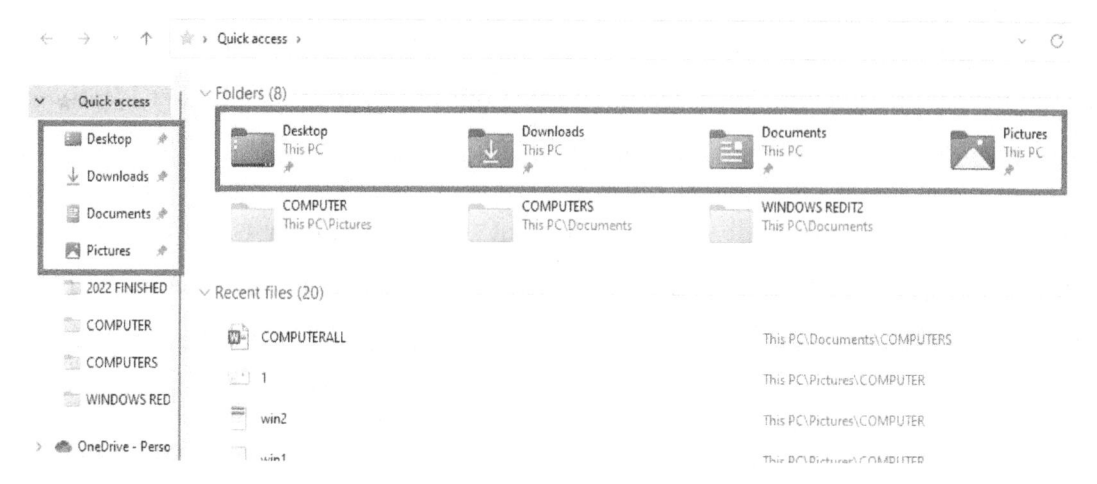

Opened File Explorer app with the major file folders indicated

Step 2

Select the folder you want to create a subfolder inside by just clicking on it for it to open.

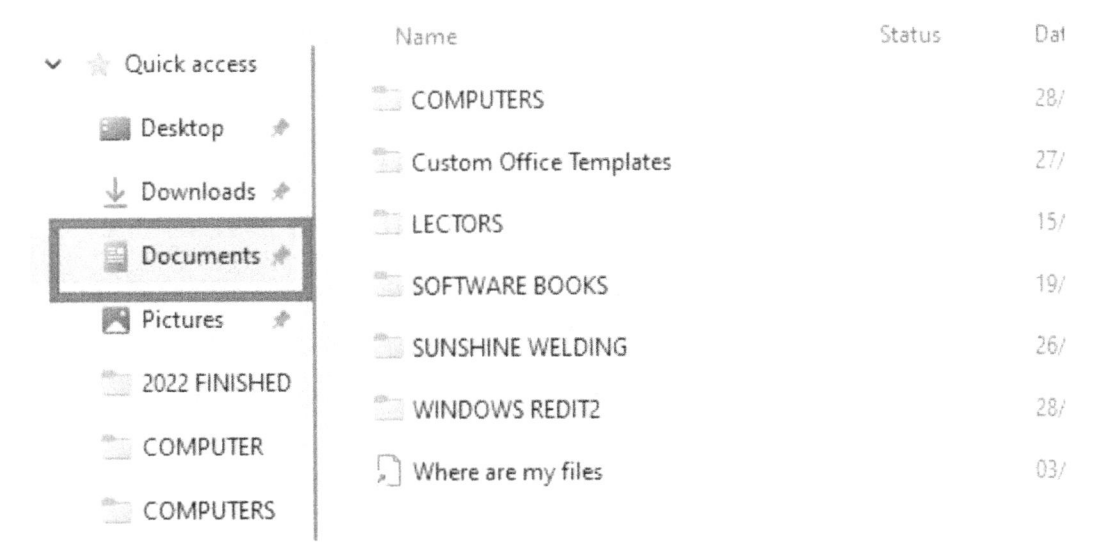

Name	Status	Dat
COMPUTERS		28/
Custom Office Templates		27/
LECTORS		15/
SOFTWARE BOOKS		19/
SUNSHINE WELDING		26/
WINDOWS REDIT2		28/
Where are my files		03/

Quick access
- Desktop
- Downloads
- **Documents**
- Pictures
- 2022 FINISHED
- COMPUTER
- COMPUTERS

Opened Documents folder for creating of subfolder

Step 3

Right-click on a free space inside the folder and some options will be displayed, and among those options, click on **New** just as you can see in the photo below.

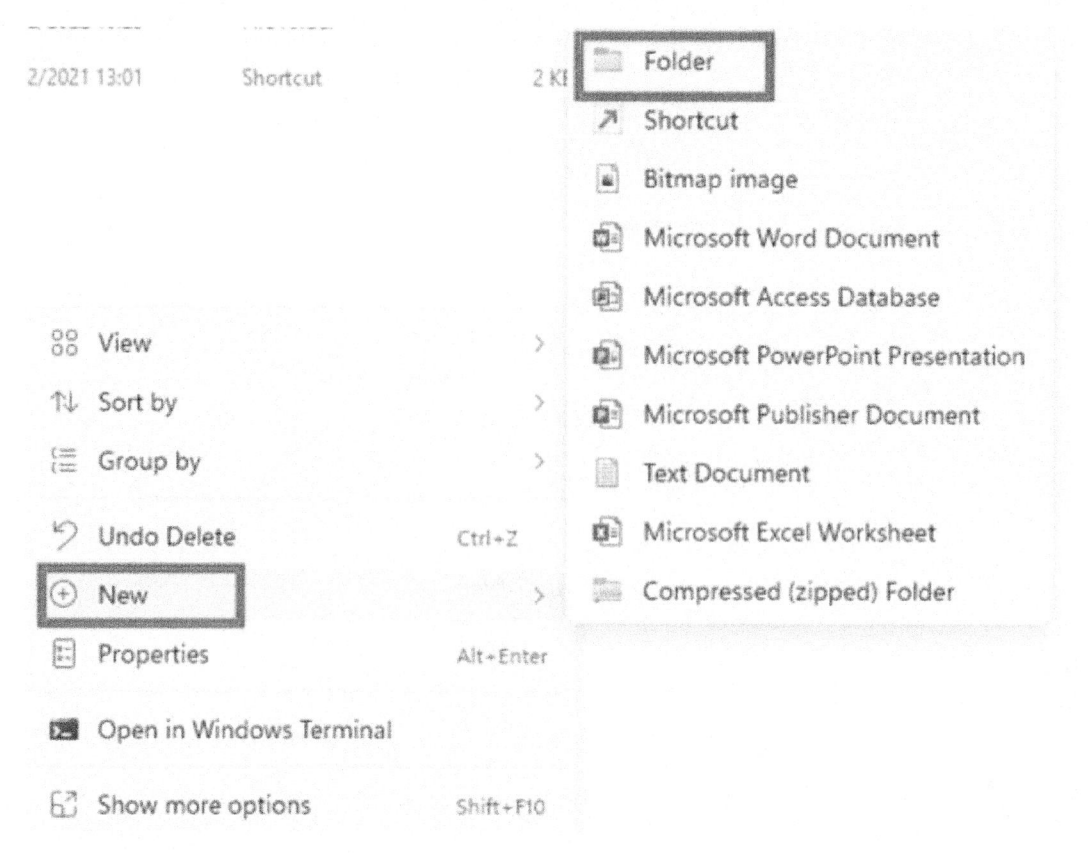

About to create a subfolder

Step 4

When you click on **New**, other options will be displayed. Just select **Folder** from the list, type the name you want to give the folder, example **SOFTWARE BOOKS**. And lastly, press the **Enter** key of your computer to save the subfolder.

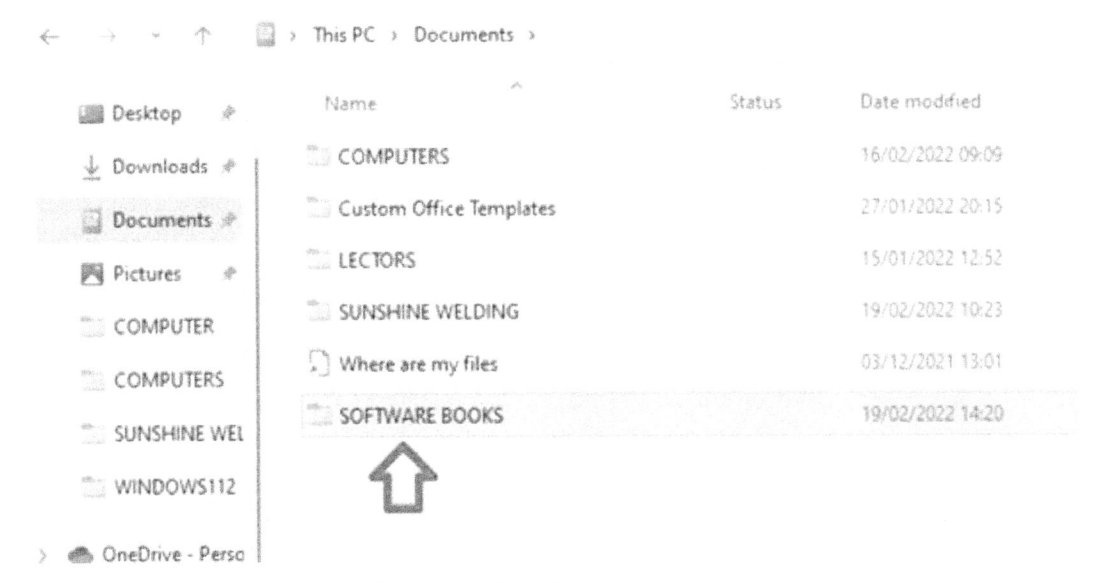

[Screenshot of File Explorer showing Documents folder with items: COMPUTERS, Custom Office Templates, LECTORS, SUNSHINE WELDING, Where are my files, SOFTWARE BOOKS]

SOFTWARE BOOKS *as the new subfolder*

With this approach explain, you can create as many subfolders as you want in your computer main folders. In addition, there are other ways you can create subfolders, but to avoid confusion, just go on with this method for now.

Copy, Paste and Cut

After creating a new subfolder, you may like to copy any file from any part of your computer and then paste the file inside the new subfolder you created. But if you do not know how to go about this, that is where there is problem. On the other hand, you may like the file existing in another folder to be cut into the new subfolder you created. When you cut any file, the file gets removed from the previous folder once you paste it in another folder or subfolder you created yourself.

To copy any file, open the folder where the file is existing and give it a click. Once you give it a click or tap it, it becomes selected. You will see some icons appear above the selected file just I have in the screenshot below.

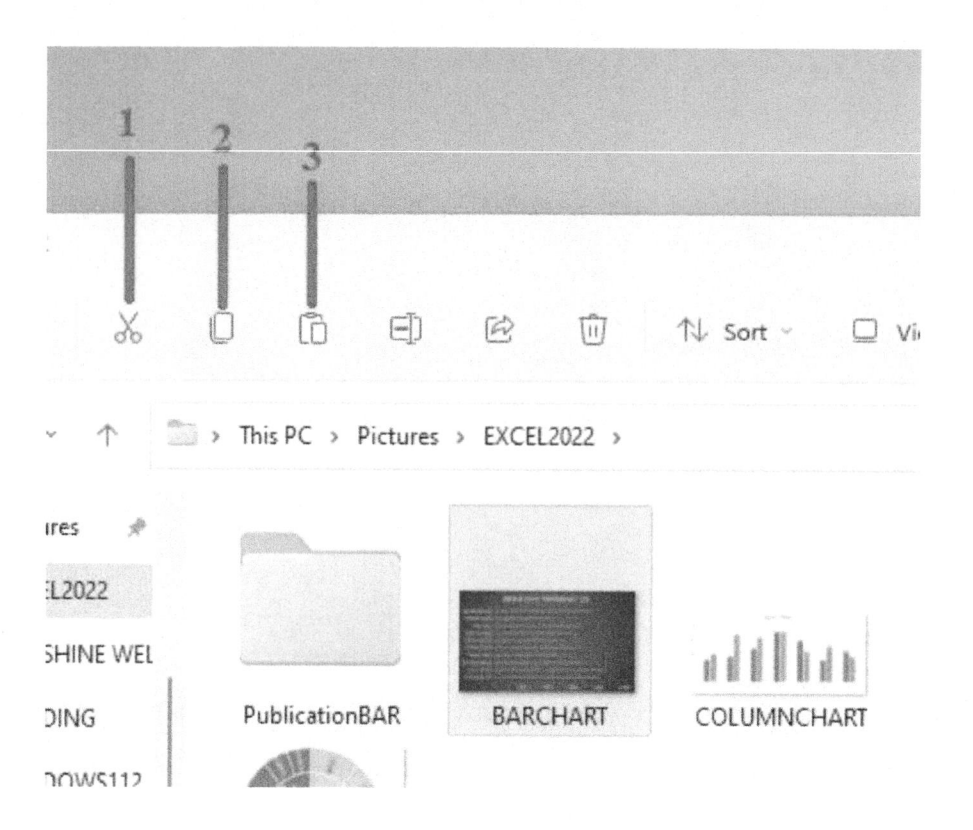

The icons for Cut, Copy and Paste respectively

If you want to copy the selected file, click on the icon labelled number **2** in the above photo. That is the **copy** icon. Open the folder or subfolder where you want to paste the file. You will see the paste icon labelled number **3** appear above the folder or subfolder. Click that icon and the file is pasted.

On the other hand, if you want to cut a file, just click on the file and then click on the **Cut** icon which is labelled Number **1** in the above photo. Open the subfolder or folder where you want to paste it, and then click the **Paste** icon which will appear above the folder or subfolder. Remember that the **Paste** icon is the one labelled number **3** in the photo above.

Adjusting Computer Screen Brightness, Flight Mode, Night Light, Battery, Keyboard Layout, Accessibility and Volume

It is nice to use computer type that is flexible. On the other hand, many users do not know how to adjust the screen brightness of their computers as well as making some changes to other features of their computers through one channel. In this part of my teaching, I will walk you through on how you can adjust the screen brightness of that your computer you are using, how to set the battery of your computer to battery saver mode for it to last longer, how to place your PC in flight mode as well as other features.

I will be giving this teaching with reference to Windows 11 OS computers, but I will still guide you on how to make the changes in Windows 10 later. So, let's keep going with making the changes on Windows 11 Operating System computers.

The first step you are to take is to click on the Quick Action Center section of your computer. The Quick Action Center is at the right bottom part of your computer screen, the same line of the taskbar section. You can click the Volume icon or the Battery icon at that bottom-right to open the Quick Action Center section which is what is displayed in the photo below.

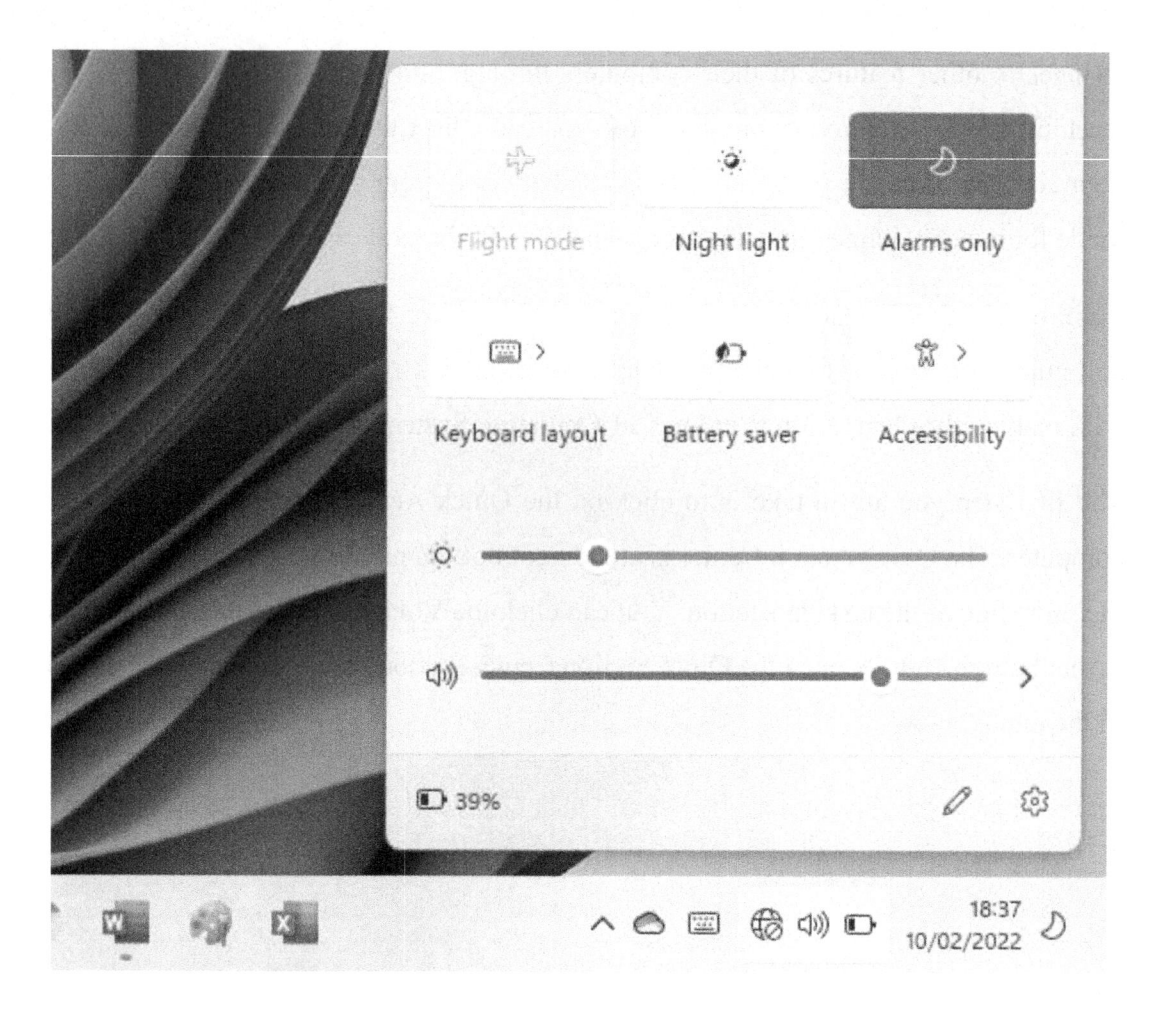

The Quick Action Center of Windows 11 OS to make some changes

Referring to the above photo, if you want to make a change on the volume level of your computer, you have to do that through the speaker/volume symbol. Place the pointer of your computer on the volume line, press and hold the left mouse button of your computer. If you drag forward through the volume line, the volume increases, and when you drag backward, the volume reduces.

On the other hand, you can increase or reduce the brightness of your computer screen. You can do that through the Quick Action Center of your computer as well. Referring to the above photo, the brightness is represented with the **Sun symbol**. To increase the brightness, press down the left mouse button and drag forward. If you want to reduce the brightness of the screen, press the left mouse button and hold, and then drag backward or towards the left. When you do that, you will see that the brightness of your computer screen reduces.

You can set your computer that is running the latest Microsoft Windows OS to flight mode. When you turn it to flight mode, the internet connection and the Bluetooth functionality is turned off as well. All you need is to click the Quick Action Center and then click the **Flight mode** icon. Once you do that, your computer is set to flight mode.

Another thing you can change through the Quick Action Center of your computer is night light feature. To turn that feature on, just click the **Night light** icon. It is important you turn it on whenever you are using your computer in the night. It reduces the amount of light that enters your eyes. In addition, when you turn it on, it makes it easy for you to fall asleep after using your computer in the night.

Alarm only is a feature you can choose through the Quick Action Center. It is a feature that when turned on, you can get some apps alarm notifications when certain things happen on your computer. An example, when you turn on your computer. Also, you can switch to other features from that icon. From that **Alarm only** icon, you can switch to other functions. You can change to **Priority only** and **Focus Assist**. When you click on the **Alarm only** icon once or twice, it switches to another function. **Focus Assist** for instance is a feature that when turned on allows you to focus on what you are doing at that moment without distraction from any form of notification that may come from your computer when working on a particular thing.

Keyboard layout is another feature that you can see in the Quick Action Center section of your computer. When you click on that option, you will see the kind of keyboard layout you are using on your computer current and the language it is modelled in.

Battery saver allows you to turn your computer to battery saver mode. When you click on that icon, all the background apps that may be making your battery to go down quickly are turned off. In a nutshell, turning on the battery saver mode of your computer will make your computer battery to last longer.

Accessibility as you can see in the above photo is another feature under the Quick Action Center of any computer running Windows 11 Operating System. When you click on the Accessibility icon, you will see some functionalities you can add to the Quick Action Center for easy access.

With the information presented in this subheading, I believe you have learned how you can make some changes on your Windows 11 computer that has to do with brightness, volume level, accessibility, battery saving and the rest. The next is to guide you on how to make related changes if your computer is running Windows 10 Operating System.

Screen Brightness, Volume, and Focus Assist in Windows 10 Computers

If your computer does not run Windows 11, you may not be able to access the features I explained in the previous subheading through the same channel. That is the reason I decided to create this new subheading for those using Windows 10 Operating System.

To adjust the volume level of any computer running Windows 10 Operating System, the first step you are to take as your computer is powered on is to click the Volume icon that is at the bottom-right of your computer screen. This is illustrated in the photo below.

About to adjust volume level of Windows 10 computer

As you click the Volume icon indicated in the above photo, you will see the volume level your computer is set at. You can drag forward to increase this volume level or backward to reduce the volume level.

Also, you can adjust the brightness of your computer that is running Windows 10 OS. To achieve that, click at the Search icon pinned at the taskbar of the computer, and then type the Word **brightness** inside the search space. The action will bring up some search results just as you can see in the photo below.

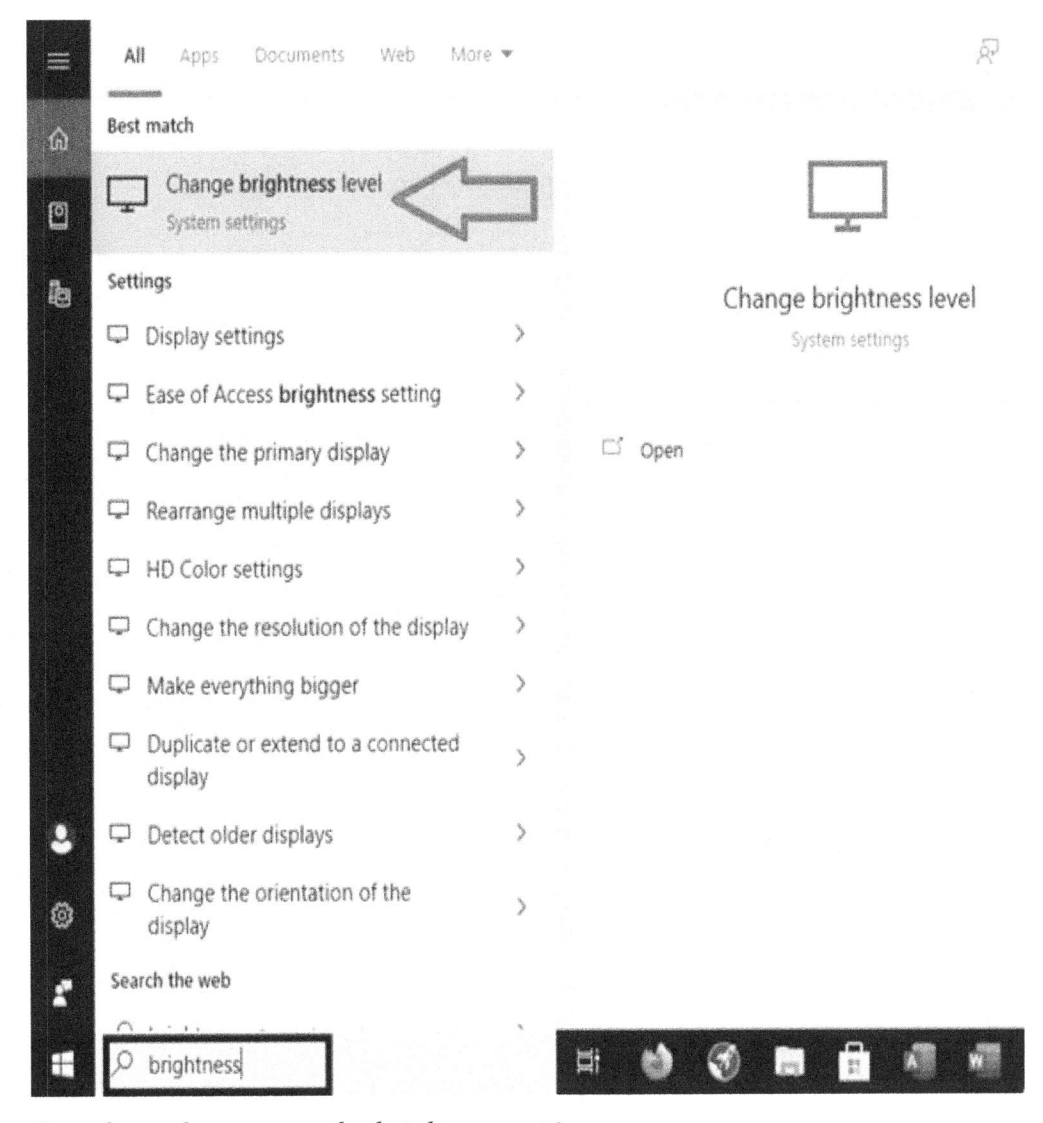

Search results to get to the brightness settings

Click on the **Change brightness level** which is indicated in the above photo. The action will open a new page indicated in the photo below.

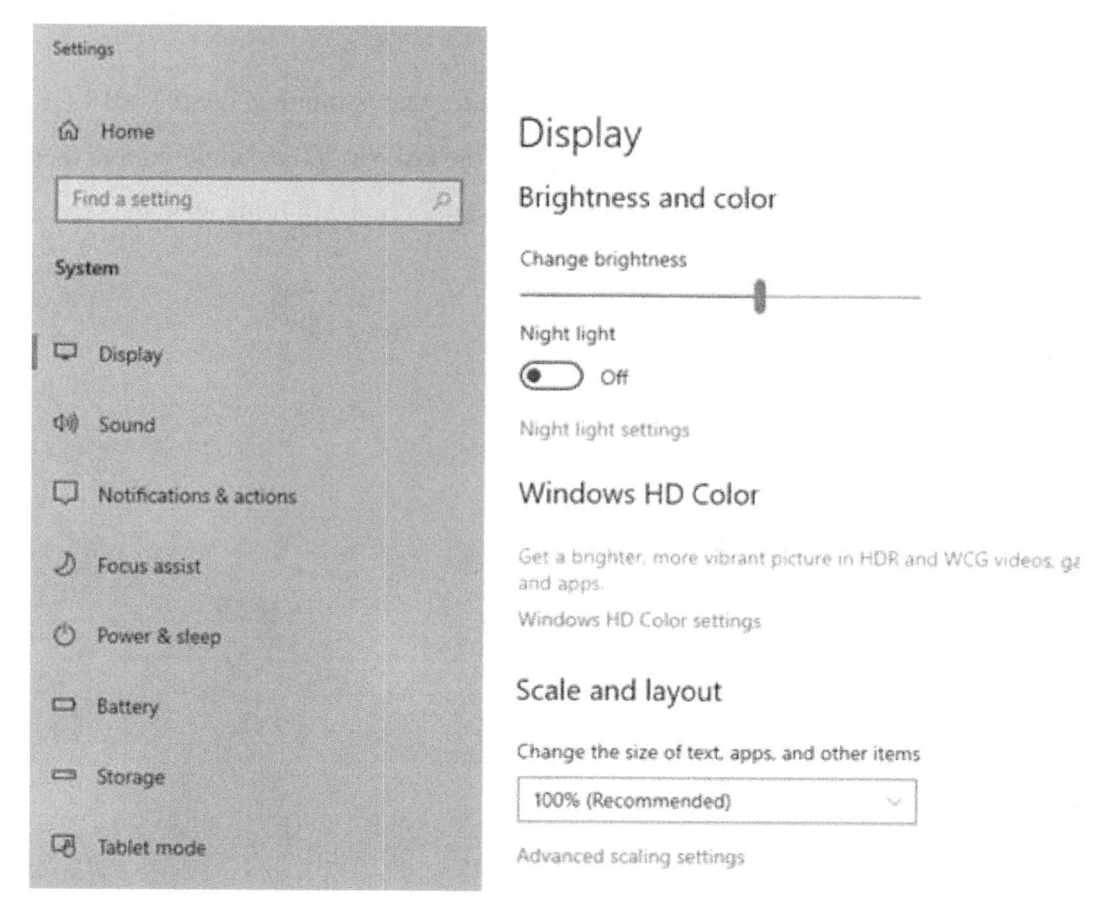

About to adjust brightness of Windows 10 computer

Under the **Change brightness**, drag through the line to increase or reduce the brightness of your computer screen.

Also, you can toggle on the button under the **Night light** to turn on the night light mode of Windows 10 computer.

Surfing the Internet with Web Browser

The internet is part of us for years now and it has come to stay. Many people's earnings for over twenty years now have been dependent on the internet. As a beginner or a senior who I assume do not know anything much on how to use the internet to complete some tasks, I will walk you through on all you have to know on surfing the net. I will be teaching you on this using Microsoft internet browser which is officially known as the Microsoft Edge.

To launch the Microsoft Edge browser, click on it as it is pinned at the taskbar of your computer by default. This is indicated in the photo below.

The Microsoft Edge browser pinned at the taskbar of a computer running Windows 11 OS

If the Edge browser is not pinned on the taskbar of your computer, click the **Search** icon pinned at the taskbar, and in the search space type the word "Edge". This action will show up Microsoft Edge browser, select it for it to be launched on your computer. In addition, if you do not have Edge browser installed on the computer you are using currently, you can download it or follow this guide with the browser that is installed in your own computer.

As your computer is connected to internet, click the Edge browser for it to be launched. You will land on the browser homepage which will look like the one I have in the photo below.

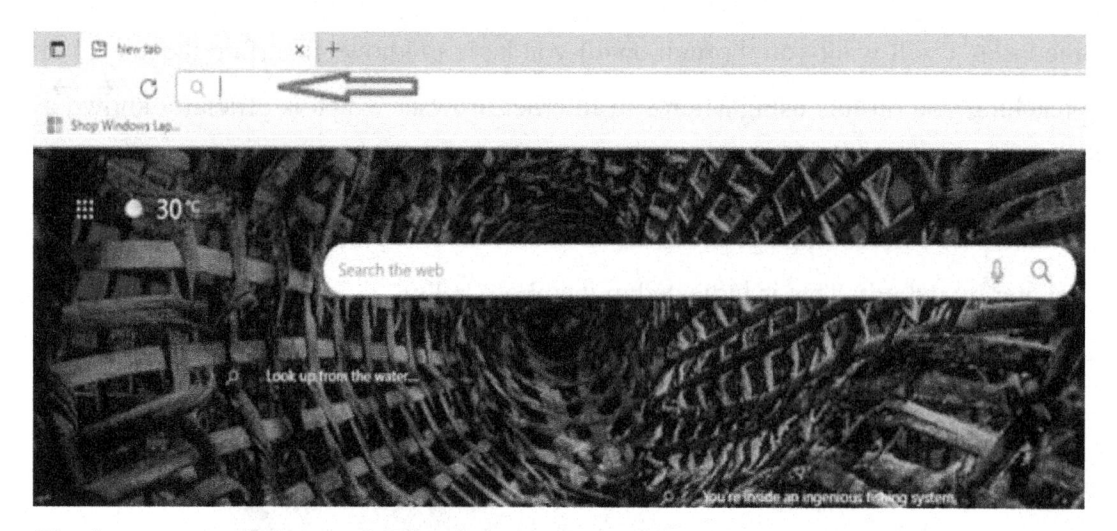

The homepage of Microsoft Edge browser

If you want to visit a website directly, just type the link to that website in the space pointed by the arrow and then press the **Enter key** of your computer keyboard. The page will load in few seconds, and you will be landed on the page. For example, if I type www.amazon.com and then hit the Enter key of my computer keyboard, the homepage of Amazon website will load. So, from there, I can access any product I want to buy from the website.

Another search section you will see when your Edge browser opens is the part that has the message **Search the web**. That is the part you can type any text and then press the Enter key of your computer to see some search results that are available on the web. For example, I can type "**the best cities in the United States**" and then hit the **Enter key** of my computer keyboard. This action will display some sources that wrote some articles on the best cities in the United States. I can then select any source of my choice by clicking on it just once. It will display some information based on that my request. After reading through that page I opened, I can go back to the search results and view the contents of the other sources. Let me go deeper on using web browser.

Accessing the History in a Web Browser
One of the things you can do in almost all web browsers is to view the browsing history. Browsing history shows you all the website links you visited in that particular browser you are using. Maybe there is a piece of information you need to access but you do not

know the exact web link that will take you to that page which you visited days or few weeks ago. Browsing history can do the job for you. It will list the website links (also known as URL) you visited in your computer browser. To get to the browsing history using Microsoft Edge browser, click the three dots that are at the top right-hand corner of the browser. The photo below shows the position of the dots.

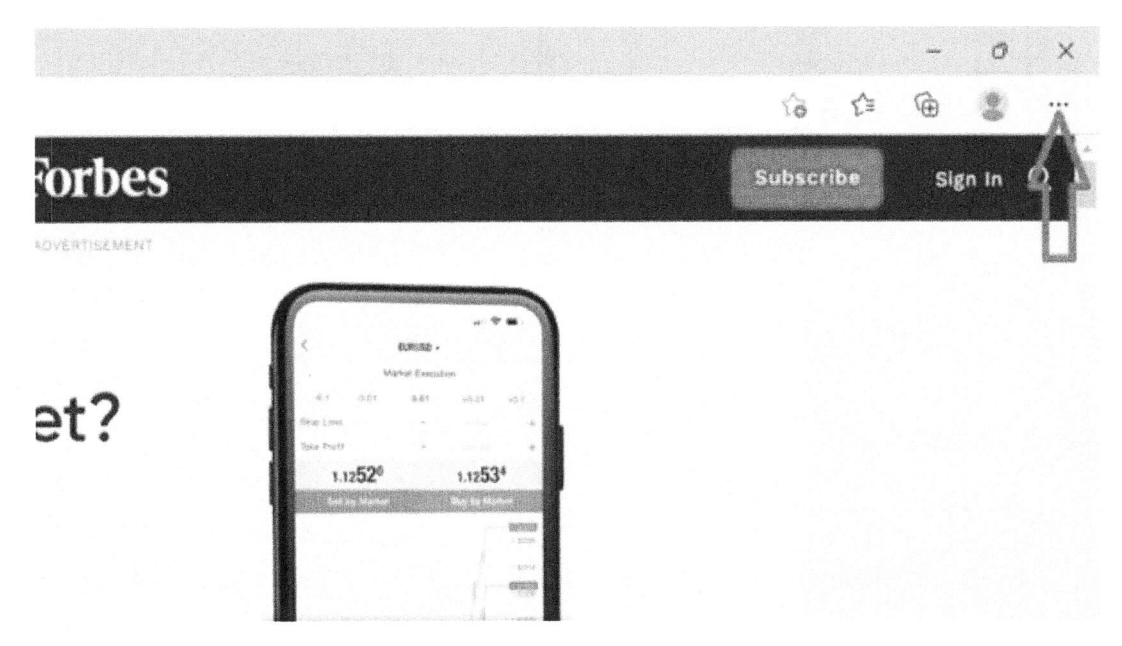

Progress in viewing browsing history

On clicking the 3 dots, you will see some options. From the options, select **History**. The History option you are to click is indicated in the photo below.

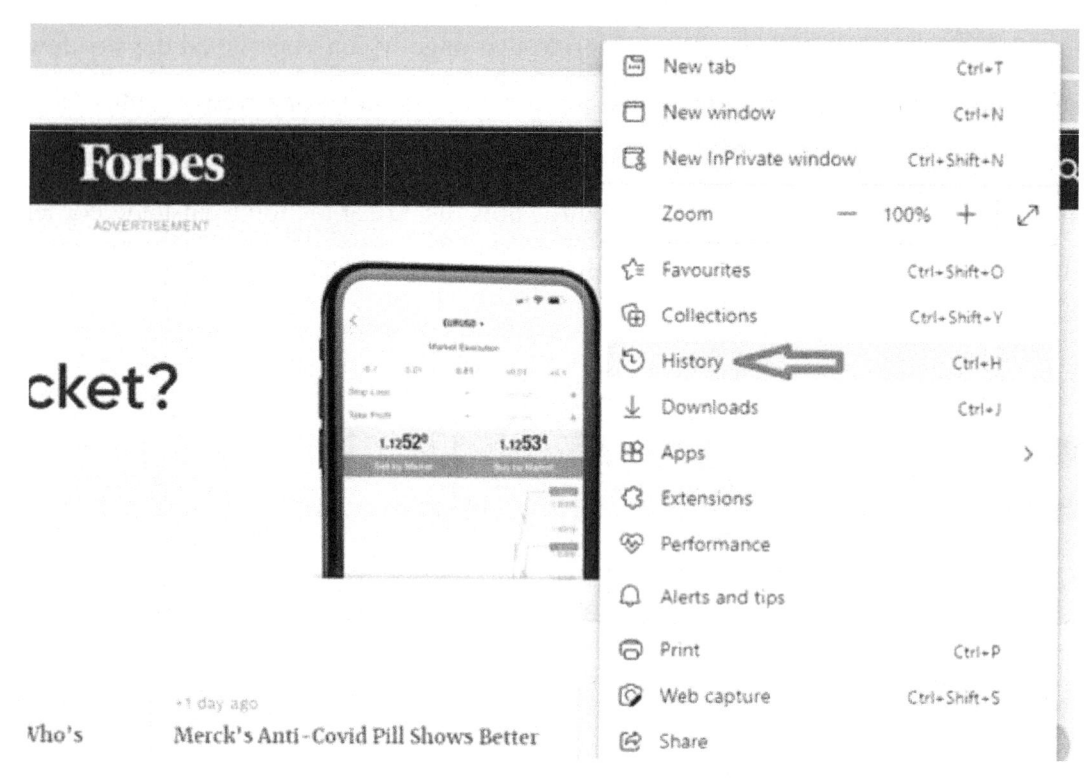

*Select the **History** command from the list*

As you click the History command, you will see some pages you visited in the browser. Sometimes, these web pages are grouped weekly and monthly. Just feel free to locate the one you want to revisit and click on it to open.

How to Add a Website to Bookmark
Sometimes, you may be browsing through a website, you feel it is important you bookmark that website. You bookmark websites you would like to be visiting some other time. To bookmark a website is recording that website for easy access in future. In a situation like that, whenever you want to access the website again, click of the Bookmark folder of the browser and you will see the websites you added to that your browser bookmark section. The next step you are to take is to click that website and it will be opened.

In some website browsers, the term "Add to Bookmark" is replaced with "Add to Favorite". So, another term used for Bookmark is Favorite. Both are pointing to the same function. Microsoft Edge for instance uses **Favorite** instead of **Bookmark**.

To add any website you will like to visit in future to Favorite, as you are on the website, click the **Add to Favorite** icon which I indicate in the photo below.

Icon to add a website to Favorite indicated

When you click on that icon, a new dialog box will show up displaying the name the website will be saved with. If you do not want to save the website with the name chosen by default, edit it. And lastly, click the **Done** button. On taking this last step, that website is added to the list other sites bookmarked in that browser.

On the other hand, anytime you want to access the website you saved in your Favorite folder, it is something simple to do. Just click on the **Favorites** icon, and it will display all the websites you added to Favorite. The photo below indicates the icon you are to click on to see all the websites you added in the Favorite folder of your browser.

Where to click to see all bookmarked websites

As you click on that icon indicated in the above photo, you will see your bookmarked websites. You can click on any of them which you make to access at that point for it to open. That is all on how you can access your bookmarked websites in your browser. Know that the position of these commands may vary depending on the computer browser you are using.

Pinning a Web Page to the Taskbar of Your Computer
Some website browsers come with beautiful features. One of such browsers is the Microsoft Edge. If you are surfing the net and come across a webpage that you like to visit again, you may pin it to the taskbar of your computer. When this is done, you can click on that webpage anytime you want to access it again and it opens. Is that not beautiful?

To pin any webpage to the taskbar of a computer, click the three dots at the top-right of the browser, click the **More tools.** This will display more options as you can see in the photo below.

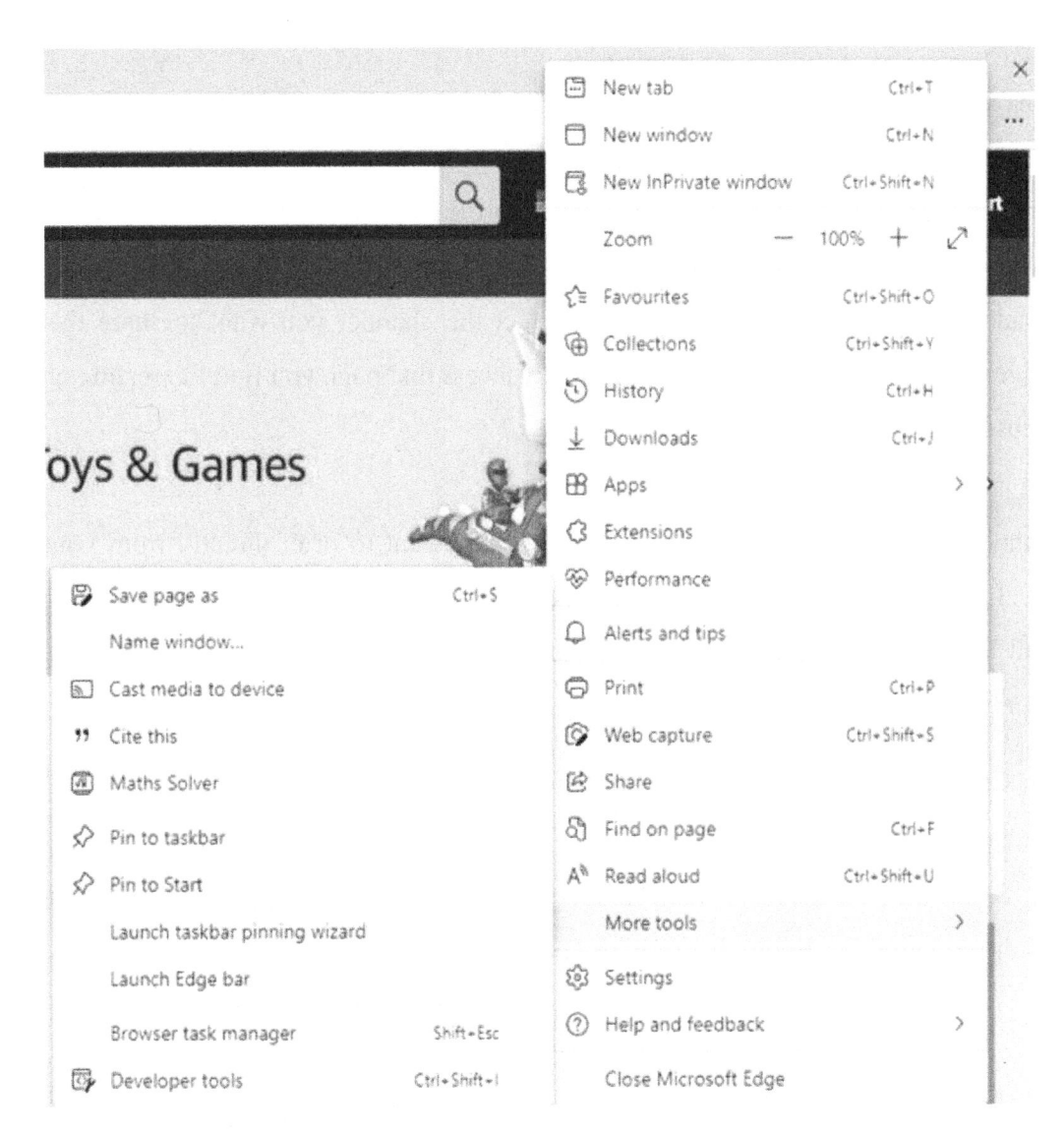

About to pin a webpage to taskbar

As you can see in the above photo, on clicking on More tools, you will see some options, so select **Pin to taskbar**. As you do that, that website page will be pinned on the taskbar of your computer.

Also, among the options is **Pin to Start**. You can click that option if you want that website page you are browsing through to be pinned to the Start menu of your computer. There are other options in that **More tools** tab which you can experiment with. Microsoft Edge browser has stunning features to help you work better and smarter.

How to Share a Web Page with Others

You may be browsing through the internet and then come across an important webpage you feel it will be nice you share with a friend. Web browsers these days make it possible for you to do so. Referencing to Microsoft Edge browser, if you want to share any website page you are browsing through, click the three dots at the top-right of the page, and select **Share** from the options. Select the channel you want to share that webpage and then send to anybody you want to access that page you find interesting on the website.

How to Print a Webpage

You may find something on the internet which you want to print directly from your printer. It is possible to do that without any stress of any kind. The steps you are to take to print any webpage using your printer are as follow (know that this is for Edge browser):

- Click the three dots at the top right corner of the browser
- Select **Print** command
- Select the printer that is connected to your computer which you want to print the information from, and then follow up with other prompts.

Accessing the Settings of Your Web Browser

There are so many things you can change through the settings of the web browsers you are using to browse the internet. Many beginners and seniors do not know about this. But for the fact that you bought this book, or a friend shared it with you, I will ensure I put you through on it. You can even change the folder where all downloads you make through the browser are saved.

To get to the Settings of your website browser, example Microsoft Edge, click the three dots at the top-right of the browser (know that the three dots are also called ellipsis). This action will display some options as usual. Scroll down until you get to the **Settings** and then click on it.

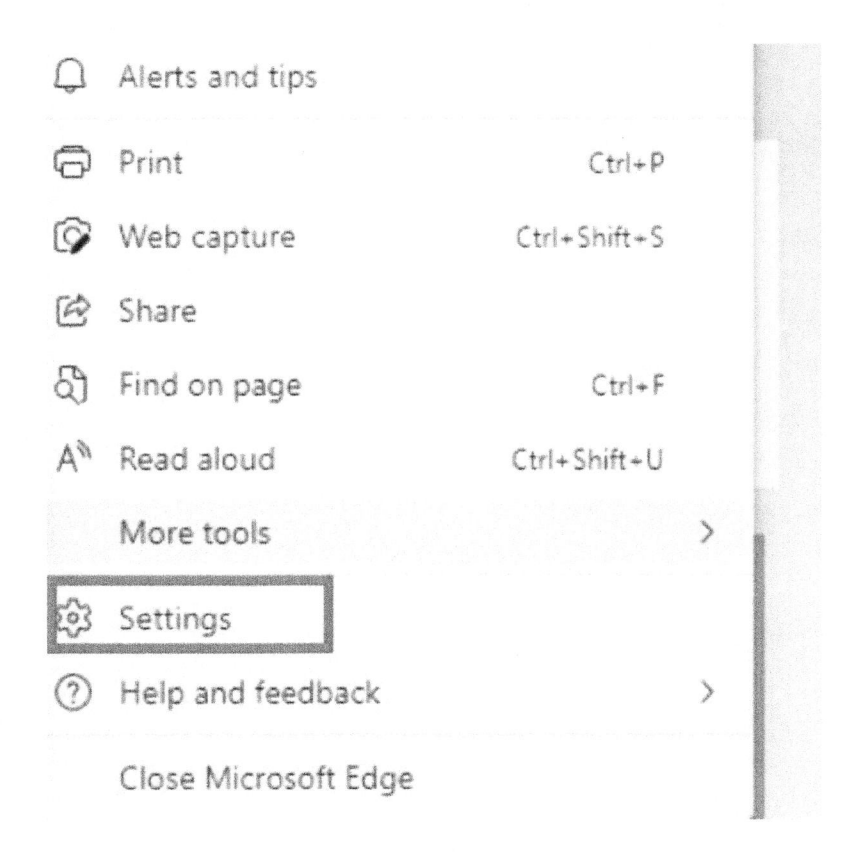

🔔	Alerts and tips	
🖨	Print	Ctrl+P
◎	Web capture	Ctrl+Shift+S
⤴	Share	
🔍	Find on page	Ctrl+F
Aⁿ	Read aloud	Ctrl+Shift+U
	More tools	›
⚙	Settings	
ⓘ	Help and feedback	›
	Close Microsoft Edge	

Settings *as one of the options on clicking the ellipsis*

As the Settings page opens, it will look like what I have in the photo below.

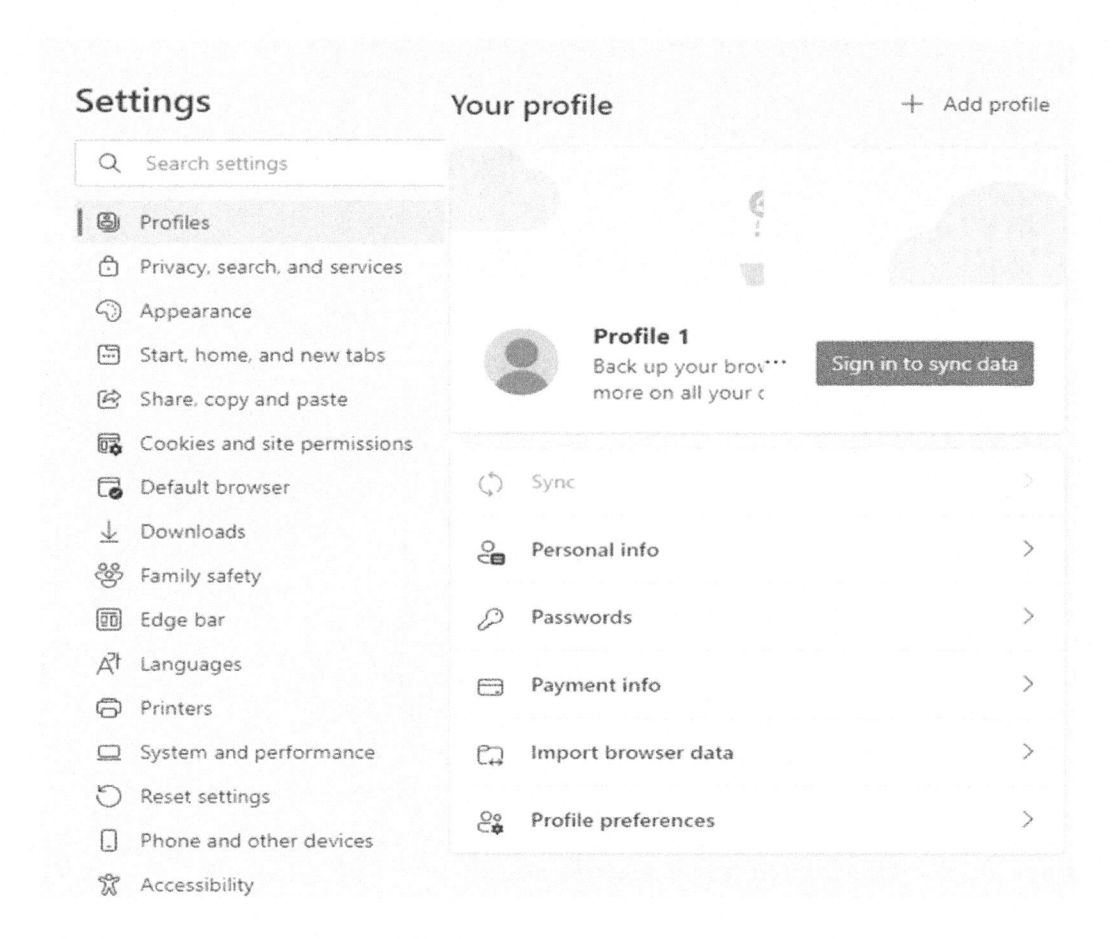

[Screenshot of Microsoft Edge Settings page showing the Profiles tab with sidebar options: Profiles, Privacy, search, and services, Appearance, Start, home, and new tabs, Share, copy and paste, Cookies and site permissions, Default browser, Downloads, Family safety, Edge bar, Languages, Printers, System and performance, Reset settings, Phone and other devices, Accessibility. Main panel shows Your profile with Profile 1 and a "Sign in to sync data" button, along with Sync, Personal info, Passwords, Payment info, Import browser data, and Profile preferences options.]

The Settings page of Microsoft Edge

As you can see in the above photo, when you click on the Settings command, a new page opens with many tabs on it. The first that you are landed on is the Profile tab. On this tab, you can sign in on the Microsoft Edge browser. All you need to do is to click **Sign in to sync data**. When you sign in, some things you do on the Edge browser on your computer will be recorded also when you use the same browser on your mobile phones. That which will be recorded are favorites, passwords, history and others. Other things you can change under the profile Settings are Microsoft Rewards, Personal info, Payment Info, Passwords, Import browser data, and Profile preferences.

Other tabs that are in the Settings of Microsoft Edge are Privacy, search, and services; Appearance; Start, home, and new tabs; share copy and paste; Cookies and site permissions; Default browser; Downloads; Family and others. Just feel free to click on any of those tabs and see the changes you can make.

Let me explain the Downloads Settings with illustrations. Through the Downloads Settings tab, you can change the folder you want any file you download from the website browser to be saved. You can structure the browser to ask you on what you want to do with the file you are downloading, Open Office file in browser, and show downloads menu when a download starts. All these you will see when you click that **Downloads** Settings tab.

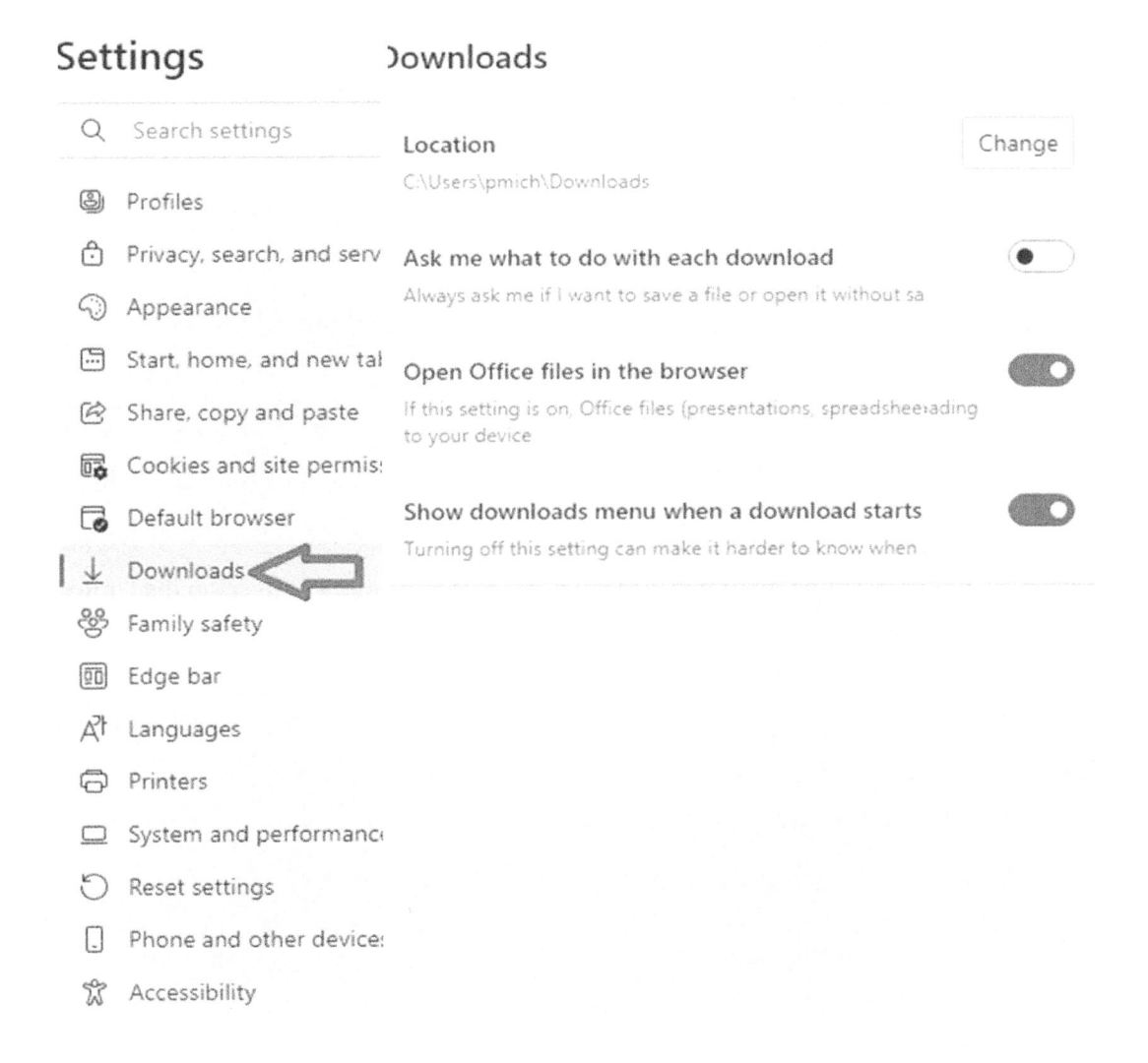

*Options available on clicking **Downloads** Settings tab*

In the above photo, the **Downloads** tab has already been selected and you can see some functions you can change from there. I want to point at the **Location**. By default, any file downloaded from the browser is saved in the **Downloads** folder created in your computer. You can choose another folder created by yourself or the one already existing in your computer as where you want anything downloaded from your web browser to be saved. To change that, click the **Change** button under that Location, and then select the folder you want any file downloaded from the web to be saved.

The Use of Email

The use of email is important because it helps in effectively communication. Whether you work in an office, companies or an individual, you are likely to use email address to send electronic mails to people in different locations. The full meaning of email is electronic mail. You communicate to your recipient electronically. I will start by walking you through on how you can create a new email address for free. After that, I will guide you on how to perform other tasks that has to do with electronic mail.

How to Signup for a New Email Address

You can only communicate with other people through email when you have an email address. If you do not have an email address, there is no way you can do that. I will be teaching you on how to create Gmail account. Know that there are other Email service companies, but I am using Gmail because it has the largest number of users in the United States of America.

In United States, 44% of people in the country use Gmail to communicate electronically. This number is followed by Yahoo Mail with 26% US users. The gap is much, and the majority carry the vote. So, I am going with Gmail which is owned and designed by Google. To open a Gmail account is free. It does not cost anything.

To create a new Gmail account, in your computer web browser, example Microsoft Edge, type the link https://accounts.google.com/signup, and then press the **Enter key** of your computer keyboard. That action will open a new website page that will look like the one I have in the photo below.

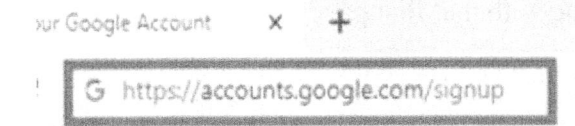

About to create a new Gmail account

Fill the details required from you. This includes your name, username, password you will be using to log into your Gmail account. In the username, type the username of your choice, example kasper2022 which Google adds the remaining part @gmail.com automatically. If after typing the name and Google detects that the username you entered is already in existence, new names will be suggested for you. So, select from the names that are suggested to you. When you are done with that first page, click the **Next** button for you to be landed on the next page just as you can see in the photo below.

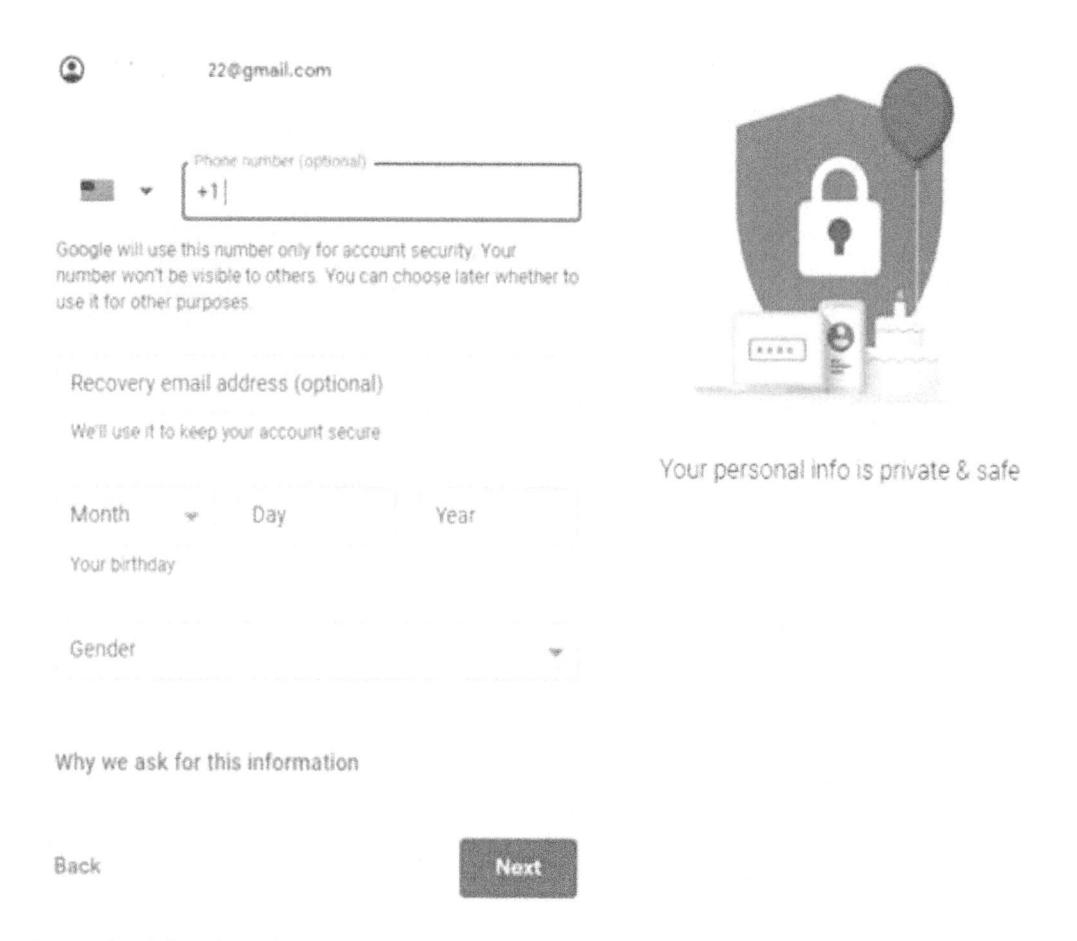

Page 2 of the Gmail account setup

From the above photo, you are required to fill in your phone number, which is optional, a recovery email which is also optional, your date of birth, and your gender. After providing the information, click the **Next** button.

On the next page that opens, agree with the Gmail terms and conditions by clicking on the **I agree** button which is at the bottom of the page.

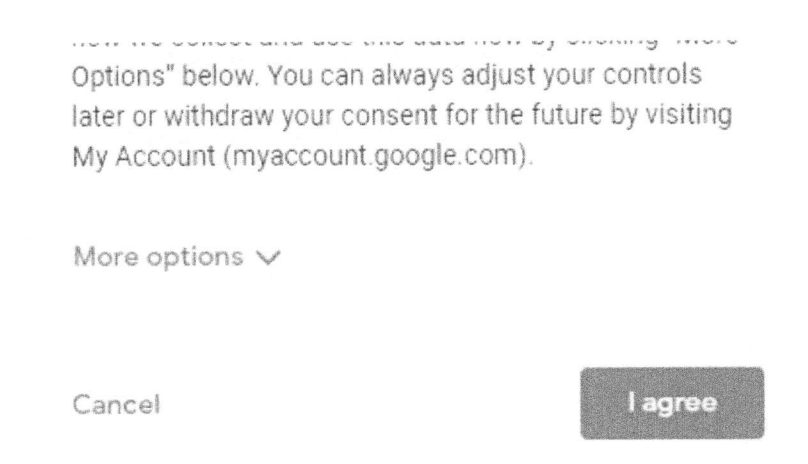

*Agree with the terms and conditions by clicking the **I agree** button*

You will be taken to a new page that will display all the Google apps you will have access to by just creating a Google Mail account. Part of the page is what I have in the photo below.

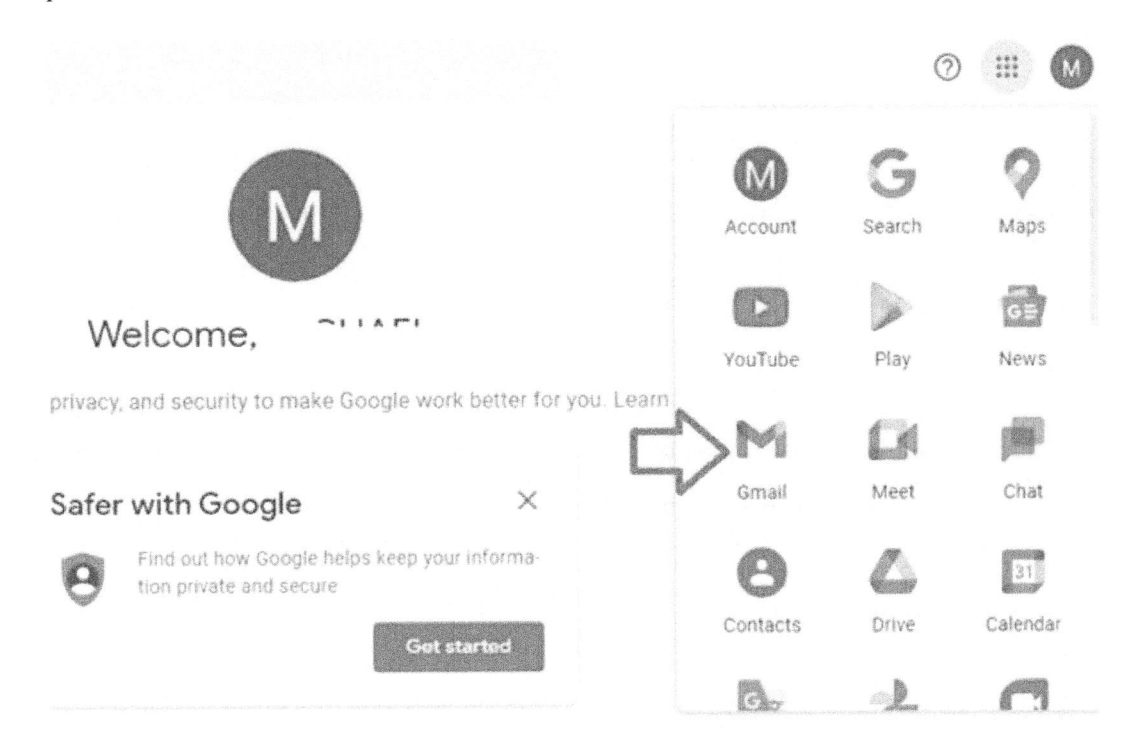

The page you will be taken to after agreeing with Google terms and conditions

Because our interest is on creating and using Gmail, just click the Gmail icon which is indicated with an arrow in the photo above. You will be taken to your Gmail inbox on doing that. The photo below will resemble what you will see.

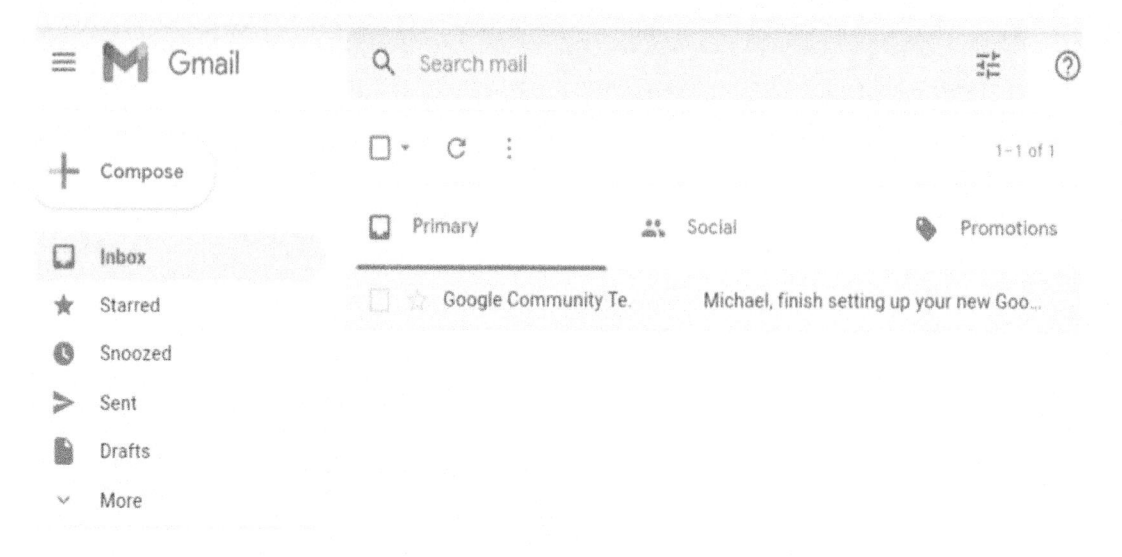

My Gmail inbox after creating a new Gmail account

How to Communicate with Your Email Address
The main reason for creating a Gmail account or any email from any company is for communication. If anyone shares his or her email address with you and tells you to send email to him or her, it is something simple to do. That is the communication. Once the email address is received by the person (he or she is called the recipient), the person may reply to you if that is needed.

To send any email to a recipient (that is, sending mail to the person), as you sign into your email account, click the **Compose** button which is positioned at the top-left corner of the Gmail interface. This will open a page that will look like what I have below.

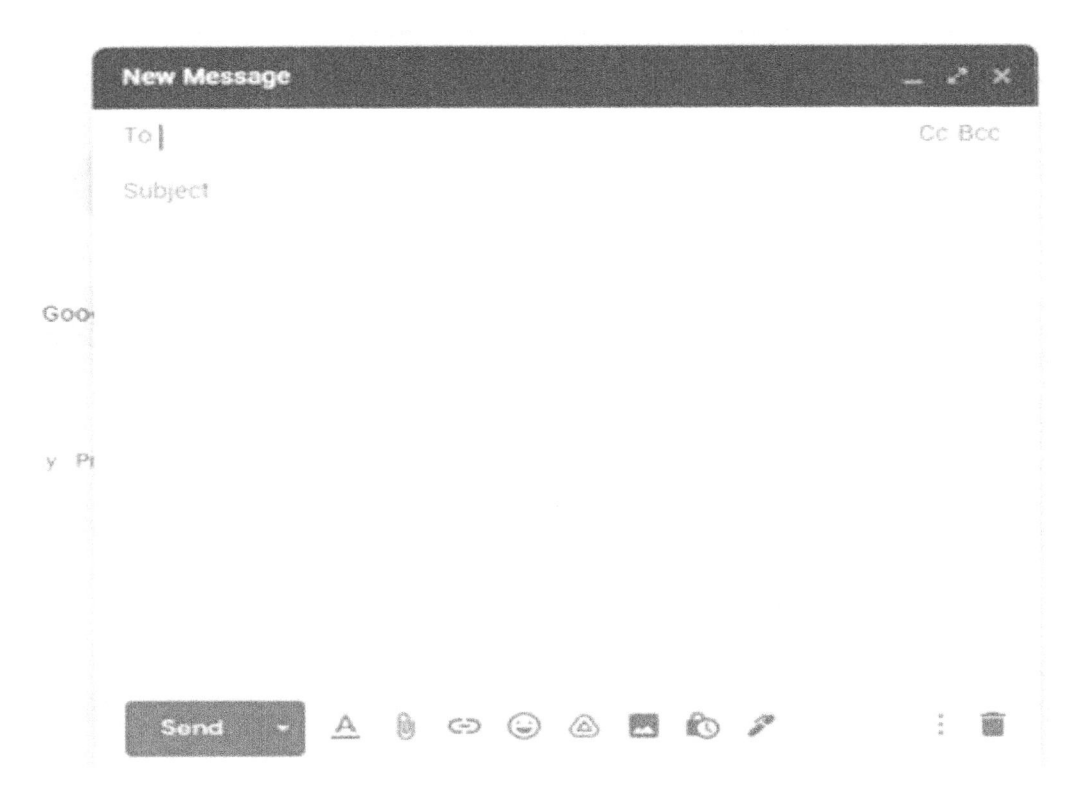

About to send an email to someone

In the space created at **To**, type the email address of the recipient, example Kellymax@gmail.com or kellmax@yahoo.com. In the **Subject**, give the email any subject that fits into what you are sending. Click the body section of the mail and detail out the message you want to send to the recipient.

After composing the mail, click the **Send** button and the mail will be sent to the recipient.

In addition, if you want to attach any document you have in your computer to the mail before sending it out to the recipient, click the **Attach icon** which is indicated in the photo below.

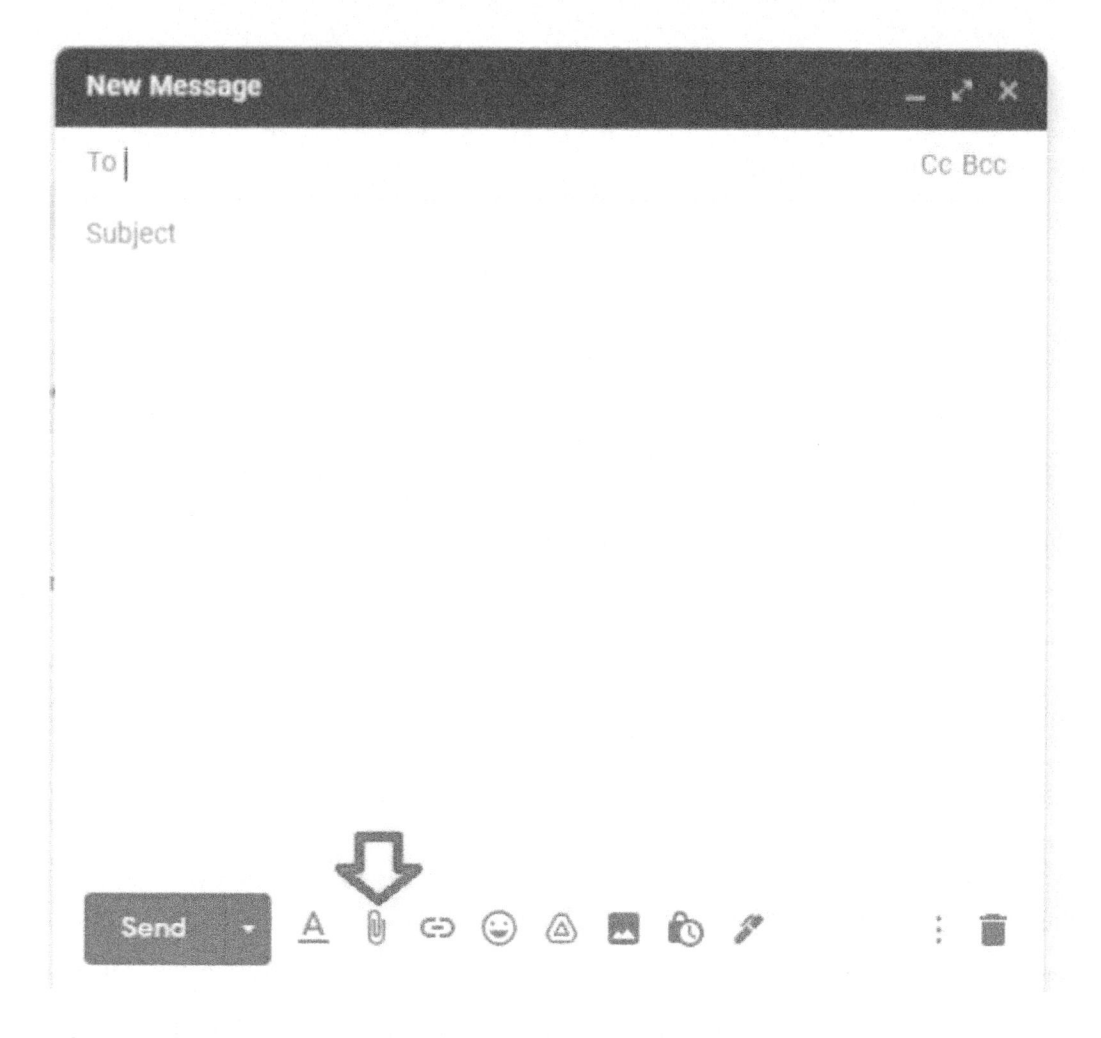

*The **Attach icon** indicated*

As you click on that icon, your computer documents section will be opened automatically. Locate the file you want to attach, and then double-click on it to be attached into the mail. Then click the **Send** button to send the mail with the attached file.

Another thing I want to let you know as a beginner or senior is how to find out if the mail you sent went through. You can check for that through the **Sent** tab. As you are logged into your computer, click the **Sent** tab which is one of the tabs at the left-hand margin of the screen. You will see some mails that you have sent out to people. Once the mail you sent appears in that section, it means the mail has already been delivered to the recipient. The recipient will see the mail when he or she signs into his or her own email account.

Another tab you will see at the left-hand margin is the **Drafts** tab. Click on that tab to see some mails you composed but did not send them out to the recipients.

Things to Know After Creating an Email Account
It is important to let you know few things after you have fully signup for the Gmail account. The first thing is safety. If you filled phone number when you were creating your Gmail account, keep it safe. This is important because if that your Email gets hacked any day, Google may send verification code to that phone number to ensure you are the true owner of the email account when you want to recover it.

Another thing I want to let you know is on how to sign in on your Gmail account. To sign in on the Gmail account that you opened using any web browser of your choice, example Microsoft Edge or Google Chrome, type the website link www.gmail.com. You will be required to sign in with your Gmail address, example kasper@gmail.com, and your password.

How to Change a Computer's Name
In chapter 1 of this book where I guided you on how to choose name for your computer during the computer setup, I informed you that irrespective of the name you chose during the setup, you can change it later. In this section I will be walking you through on how to get that done.

Click the **File Explorer** icon pinned at the taskbar of your computer. By the left-hand margin, you will see the name of your PC. The name you will see is **This PC**. Click on that name.

Right-click on the page that opens and select **Properties**. On clicking on the **Properties**, a new settings page will open. Take your computer pointer and click on the **Rename this PC** that appears at the top-right corner.

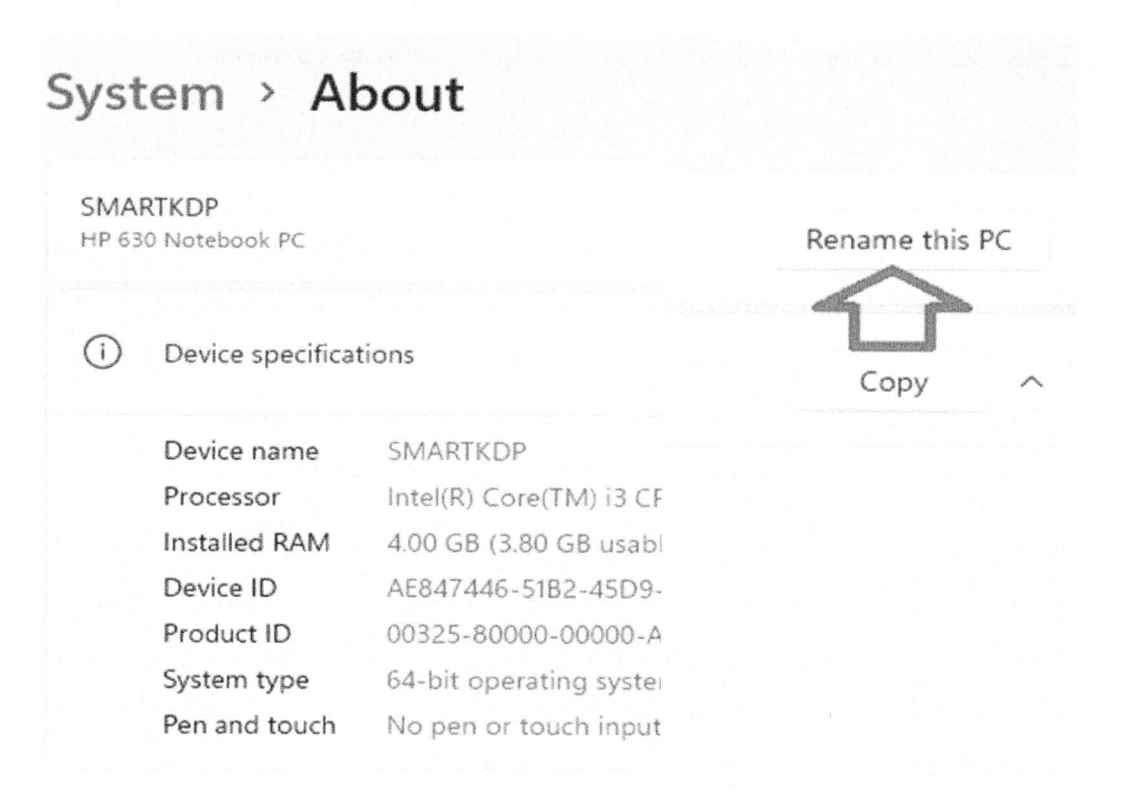

```
System  >  About

SMARTKDP
HP 630 Notebook PC                          Rename this PC

(i)  Device specifications
                                                  Copy

     Device name       SMARTKDP
     Processor         Intel(R) Core(TM) i3 CF
     Installed RAM     4.00 GB (3.80 GB usabl
     Device ID         AE847446-51B2-45D9-
     Product ID        00325-80000-00000-A
     System type       64-bit operating syste
     Pen and touch     No pen or touch input
```

*The **Rename this PC** button indicated by the arrow*

Type the new name you want your computer to be identified with, and lastly press the **Enter** key of your computer keyboard. The computer will display two options which are **Restart now** and **Restart later.** Select between the two options. Immediately you take this last step, the name of your computer will change at that moment or later if you select the option to restart later. If in the future you still want to rename your machine, take this same steps.

CHAPTER 4

MICROSOFT WORD USER GUIDE

As a beginner or a senior, Microsoft Word is one of the applications you are likely to use often in that your computer. It is one of the most used Word processor desktop app. With Microsoft Word, you can create beautiful documents. If you have touched hard copy documents which have text on them, the documents are likely to be created using Microsoft Word. Without going too far, this book you are reading right now was created using Microsoft Word app. One of the beautiful things about this software is that it is not only available for desktop computers, but you can download it into your smartphone, install it, and start using it there as well.

In one of the early chapters of this books, I walked you through on how you can get and install Microsoft 365 suite on your computer. In that teaching, I stated that once you install the program on your computer, you will have Word, Excel and other major Office apps up and running in your PC. So, for that reason, I will not cover how to install the Word app on your computer in this chapter. I have done that already. Also, if you have Microsoft Word already installed on your computer, you will follow up properly in this teaching. I will teach you all the important areas of Microsoft Word you need to know to excel in the use of the app.

Launching Microsoft Word
If your Microsoft Word app is pinned at the taskbar of your computer, what you are to do for it to be opened is just to click on the Word icon and it will be launched. Please know that another name for "Microsoft Word" is just "Word". So, do not get confused when I use the short form of the name.

On the other hand, if the Word app is not pinned at the taskbar of your computer and you want to get it opened, just click the **Search icon** at the taskbar of your computer, and then type "Word" in the search bar. This action will bring up the Word app just as you can see in the photo below.

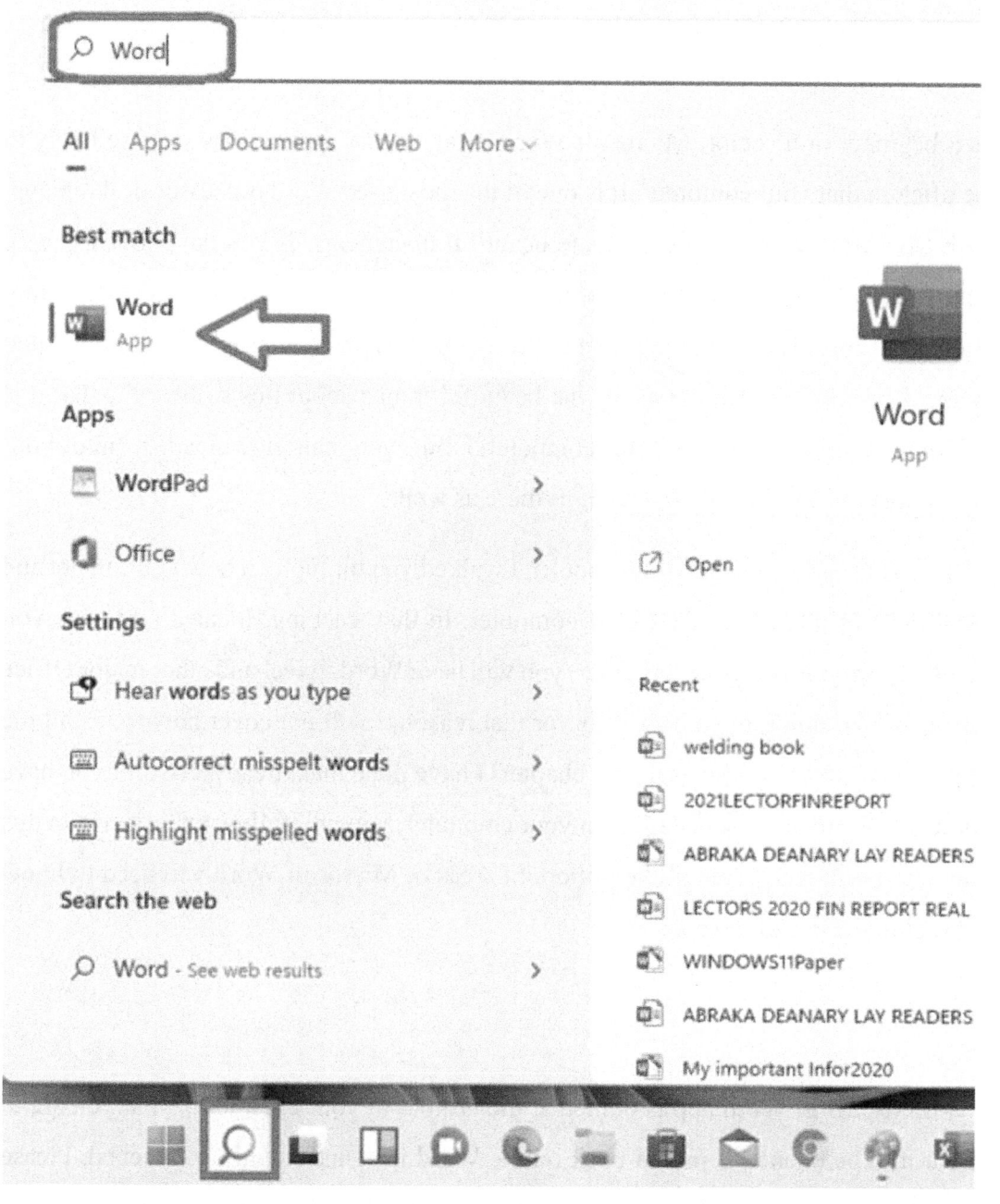

About to launch Microsoft Word app

As you can see on the above photo, just click on the Word app and it will get opened. When it opens, you will see a page that looks like the one displayed below.

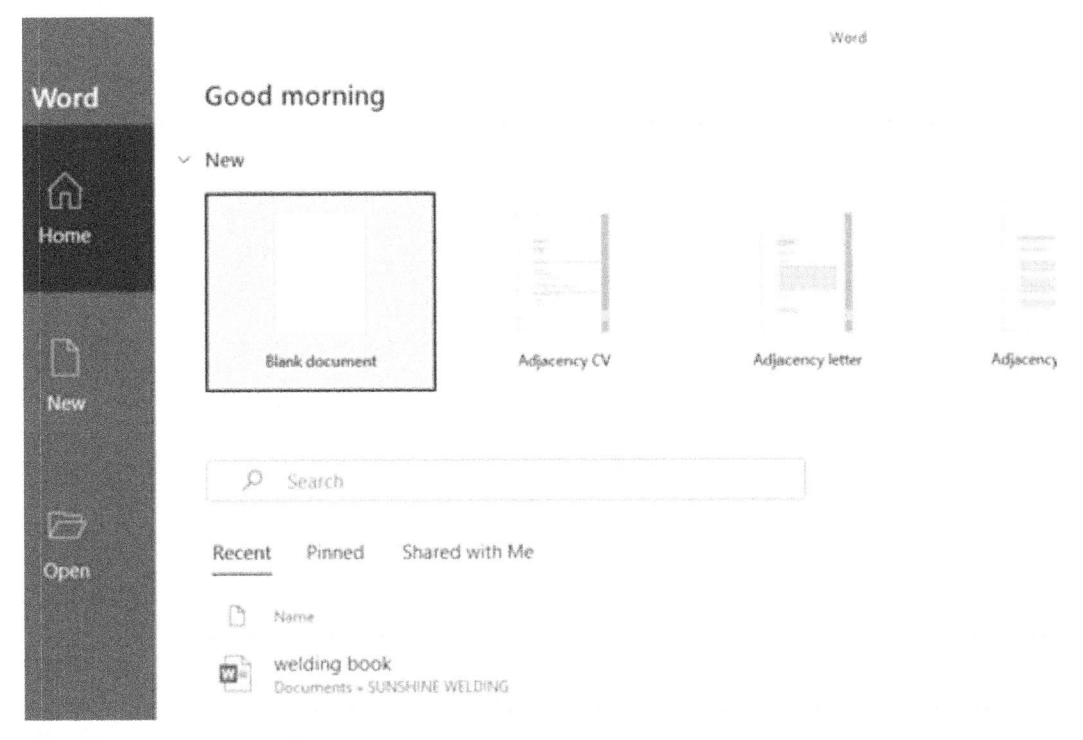

The first page you will see when the Word app opens

There are blank document and the prebuilt templates from which you can start creating your document from. An example of a prebuilt template with respect to the above screenshot is the one named **Adjacency CV**. You can select it if you want to create a CV document and then make the necessary changes to suite into what you want to have as your own document.

Another thing I want to bring to your notice with respect to the above photo is the **Recent** tab which you will see once you launch the Word app. That section displays all the documents you recently accessed. So, anytime you launch your Word app and want to continue from the document you worked on previously, it is possible to see the document under the Recent tab. Click on that document and it will open, and from there continue your typing or editing.

For the purpose of this teaching, I will be working with the Blank document. This is because most of the works you will be doing as an individual or someone targeting any office job will be based on blank document from which you build your own content. So, click on **Blank document** for it to open. As it opens, the interface you will see will look like the one displayed in the photo below.

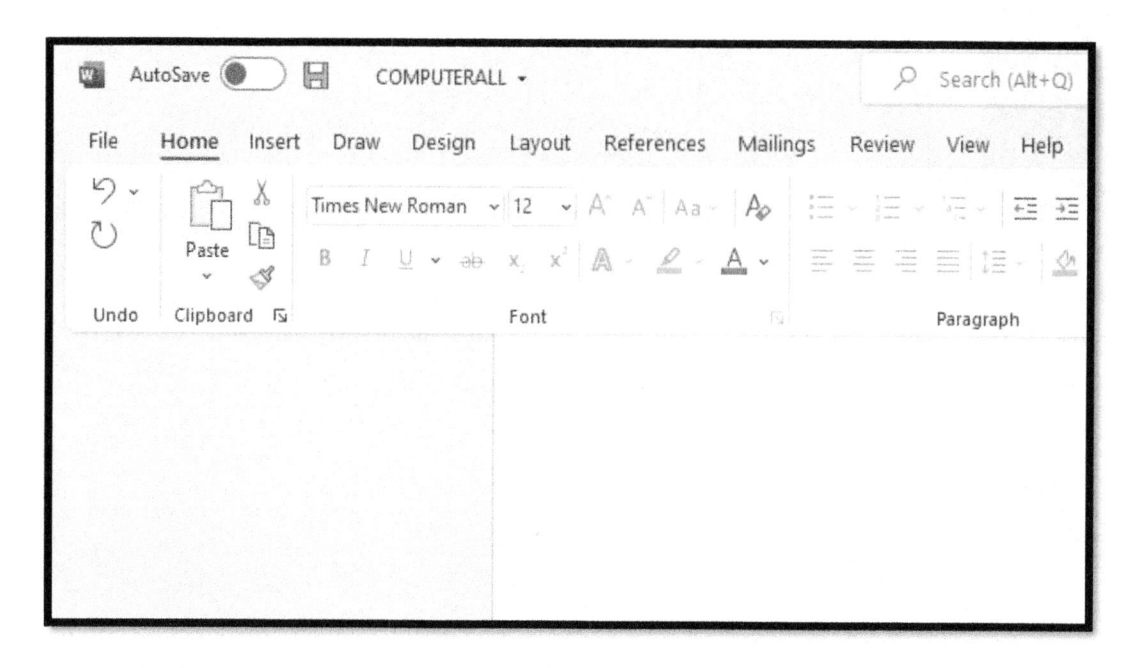

The Microsoft Word interface for composing of the document contents

Working Smart in Your Document
It is important you work smart when you type in your Microsoft Word document. For you not to work in vain, when you type in the document, always click the **Save icon** at the top-left of the Word app. The Save icon is indicated in the photo below.

*The **Save icon** of Word app indicated*

Alternatively, you can use keyboard shortcut to save the document. The keyboard shortcut is **Ctrl + S**. When you press these two keys on your computer keyboard, the document is saved. If you do not save your document after typing for few minutes, and your computer shuts down on its own due to low battery, you may lose the text you recently typed.

Though in some cases, the document may be saved in auto recovery of your Word app. But, sometimes it may fail. To be on a safer side, after typing for few seconds, save the document by yourself by clicking the Save icon or using the keyboard shortcuts.

Making Text Bold

After typing some text in your document, you may like to make some bold. The words may be the subheading part of the entire words you typed in the document. To make any text bold, highlight the words by pressing down the left mouse button and then drag through the words.

The next step for you to take is click the **Home** tab and then click the **Bold** icon which is indicated in the photo below.

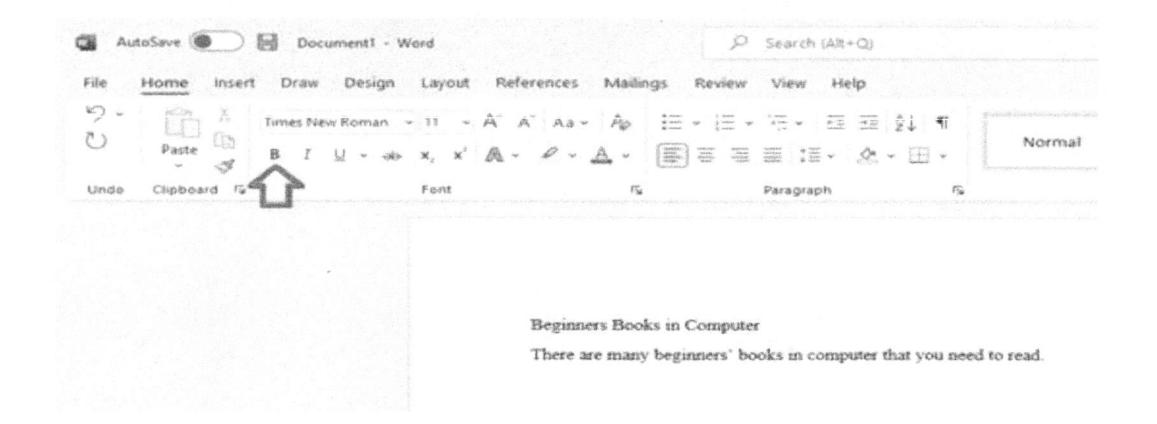

Bold *icon of Microsoft Word indicated*

On taking this last step, the entire selected text is turned bold. Use this approach to make words bold in the Word app.

Capitalizing Words in a Word Document

Sometimes, there may be some text you want to make capital in a document you have created. But if you do not know how to do that, it may be a problem. You can capitalize text by choosing the correct tool that will give you the result you need.

To capitalize all text, highlight the text and then click the **Home** tab of your Word. The next step is to click the **Change case icon**, and then select the capitalize option you want.

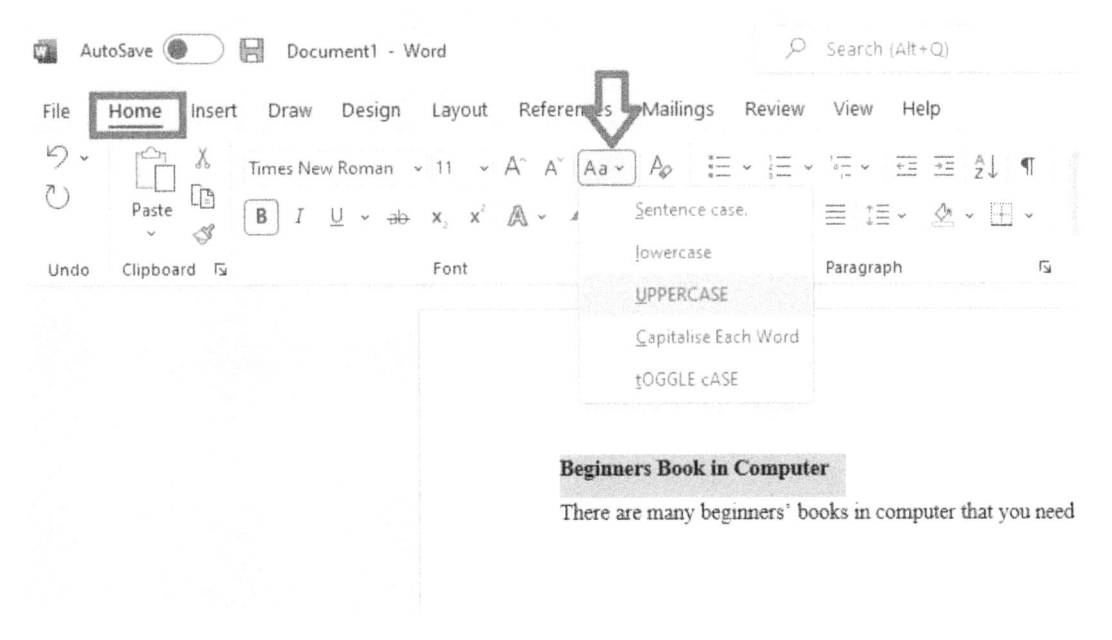

Progress in choosing a case for capitalization

From the above photo you have some options which are Capitalize Each Word, CAPITALIZE, lowercase and others. Just make you choice and the change is applied to the text immediately.

How to Insert Pictures in Word

There are some documents that when creating you need to add pictures to pass your message to the readers. If you do not know how to insert the Pictures, that is where you may have issue. This book you are reading right now has many photos in it and I inserted these photos in the document before the final publication.

To insert any picture in a Word document, take your computer cursor to the spot you want the picture inserted and click on it. As the cursor blinks there, click the **Insert** tab.

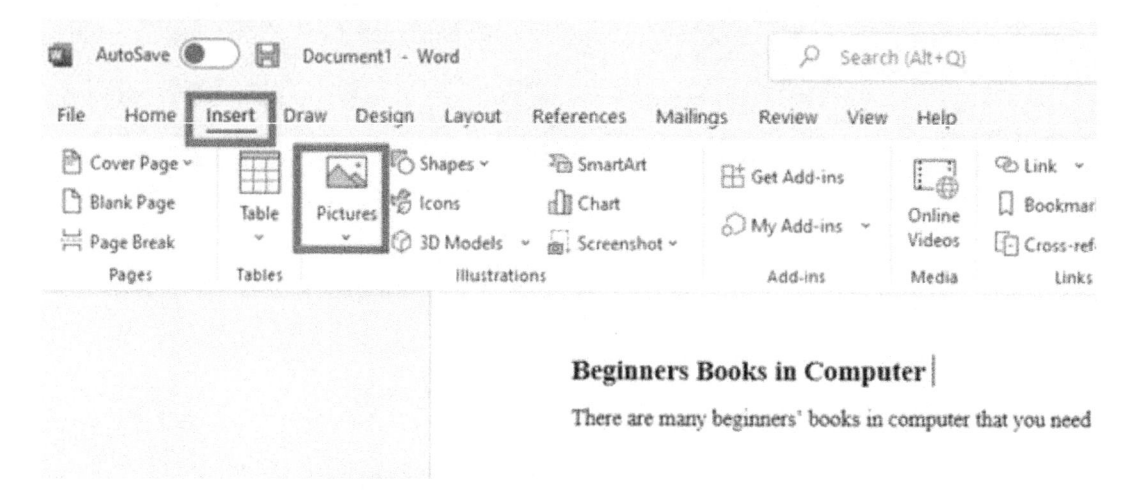

*The **Insert** tab and **Pictures** command indicated*

The next step you are to take is to click the **Pictures** command. On taking this step, your computer becomes accessed by Word. Navigate to any folder of your computer where the photo you want to use is, and then double-click on the picture. On taking this last step the picture gets inserted in your document.

Beginners Books in Computer

There are many beginners' books in computer that you need to read.

The photo showing the inserted picture in a document

How to Resize Pictures

In some cases, after inserting some pictures in your document, the picture may appear bigger or smaller that you expect. In a situation like this, you need to adjust the picture. To do this, click on the picture for it to be selected. Take the cursor to the top-right corner of the selected picture and drag downward for the size to be reduced gradually. If you want the size to be increased, just drag outward.

How to Underline Words

As of my days of primary school education, after my teacher is done writing a title, she underlines the title with chalk. Microsoft in their wisdom integrates that approach in designing their Word app.

If you want to underline some words you have already typed in a Word document, take these steps:

- Highlight the words you want to underline
- Click the **Home** tab
- And lastly click on the **Underline** command which I indicate in the photo below.

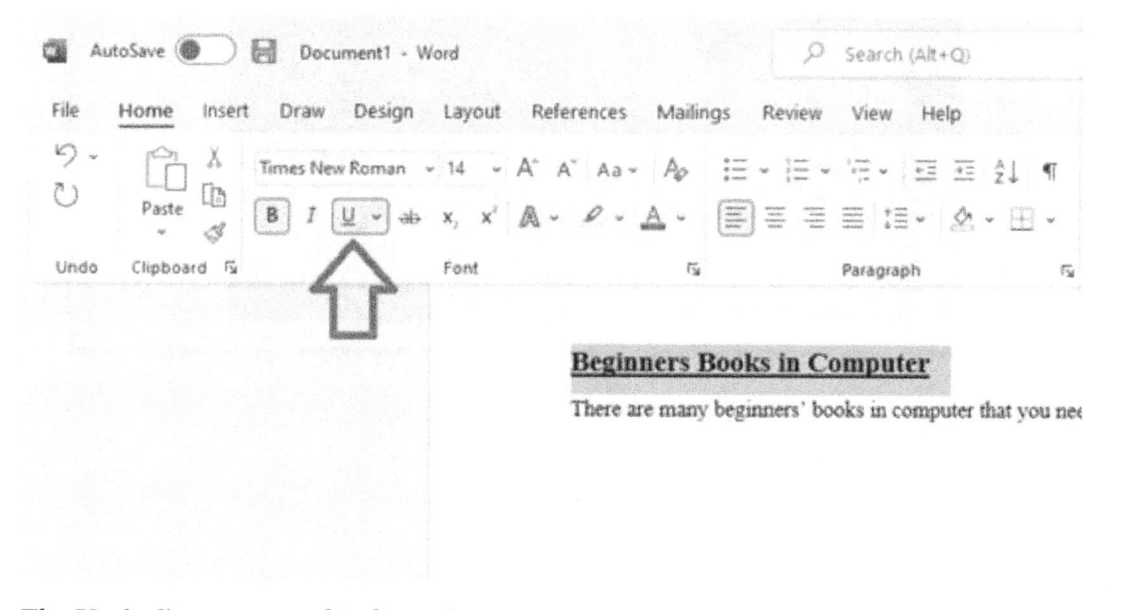

*The **Underline** command indicated*

On taking this last step, the initially highlighted words will get underlined

Finding Out the Words Count in a Document

As of those days in my university, I engaged in many essay competitions. Each of these essay competitions come with guidelines. One of the contents of the guidelines is the maximum number of words you are to type. If you composed words that are more than that given instruction, that means you had gone against the rule. And you know what that means? No judge is going to attend to your manuscript when submitted.

In respect to this, will you start counting the number of words you have typed manually? That will be a big stress. Microsoft Word has word counting tool, but many beginners and seniors do not know about this. Let me guide you on how to get to the tool that counts the words automatically.

Click the **Review** tab of your Word app. This will bring up some commands. Just click on **Word count**. This is Illustrated in the photo below.

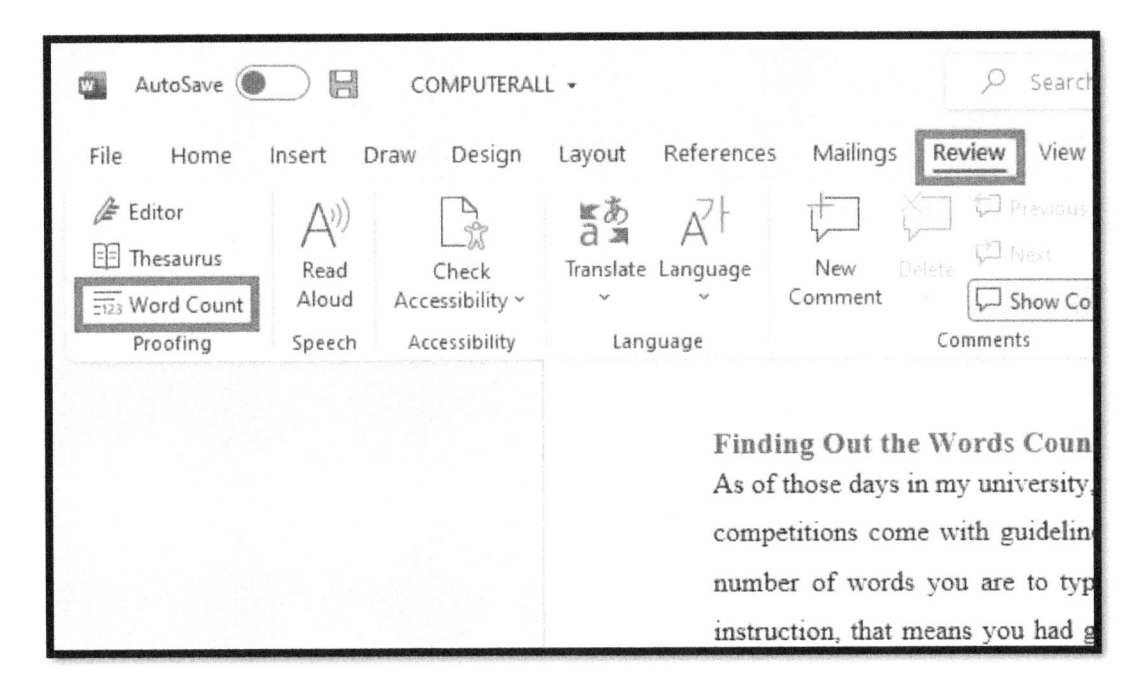

Review tab and Word count command indicated

On clicking on the **Word count** command, you will see the number of words that are already typed in that document. It is automatic and it is easier than manual counting which you are likely to make mistake when applied.

Changing Font Styles in Document

There are different types of fonts that Microsoft added in their Word app during the development of the software. With font, the text of your document is changed in terms of styles. It changes its look. I composed this book using *Times New Roman* font type. Another writer can choose to format his or her own book with a different font. Whichever font style an individual wants to use in creating his or her document is left to the person. But, there are different kinds of fonts suitable for different kind of book.

To change the font of text in a document, the first step is to highlight the text you want to change the font. Click the **Home** tab. Click on the **Font** styles command. This is indicated in the photo below.

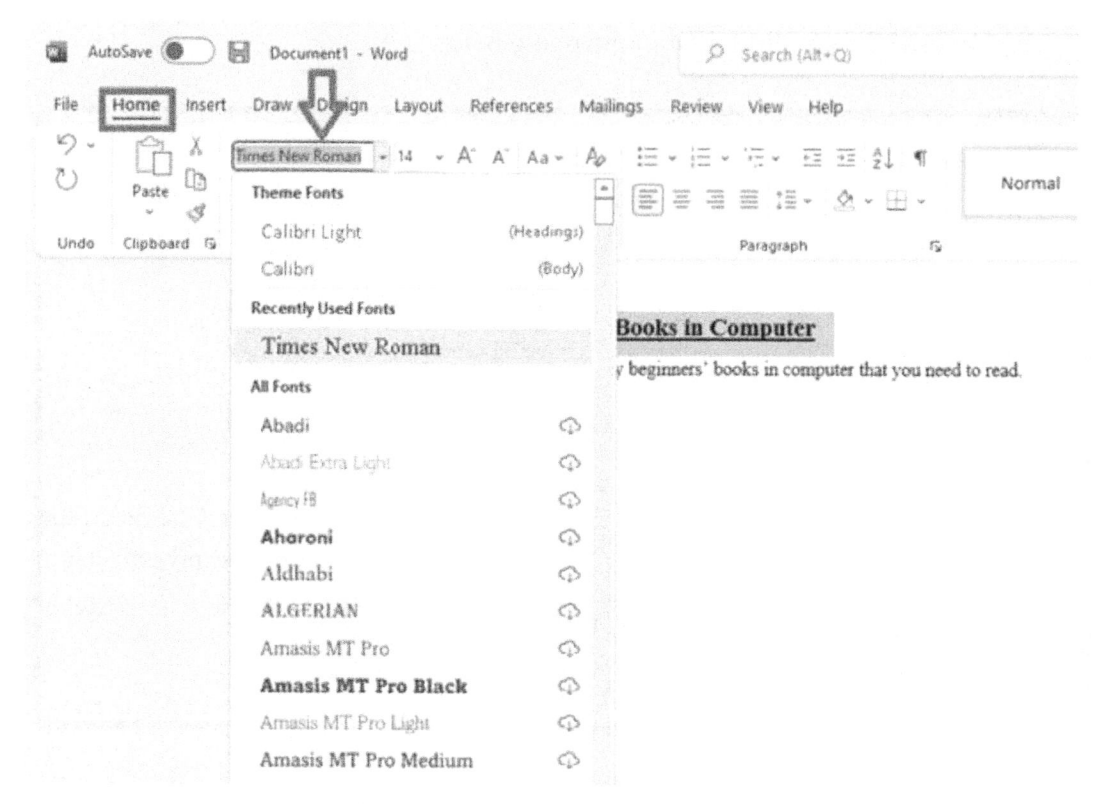

Home *tab indicated with* ***Font style*** *command pointed by an arrow*

You will see many font styles. They are so many. So, scroll down or up and select any font style you want to apply to the selected text. Anyone you click on will be applied to the text.

How to Change Text Size

Sometimes, it is necessary for all the words you have in a document to have different text size. This text size is known as font size. I used text size because I know you are a beginner or a senior and because of that may not understand some technical terms properly.

In your document, you may like to make some headings or subheadings to have bigger text size than the other parts of the document. That is what usually differentiate them from the other parts of the document. In a situation like this, you can make the text bold at first before changing the text size.

To change the font size (that is the text size), click the **Home** tab, and then click the **Font size** command. You will see the font size numbered from 8 to higher. The bigger the number you select, the higher the size of the text.

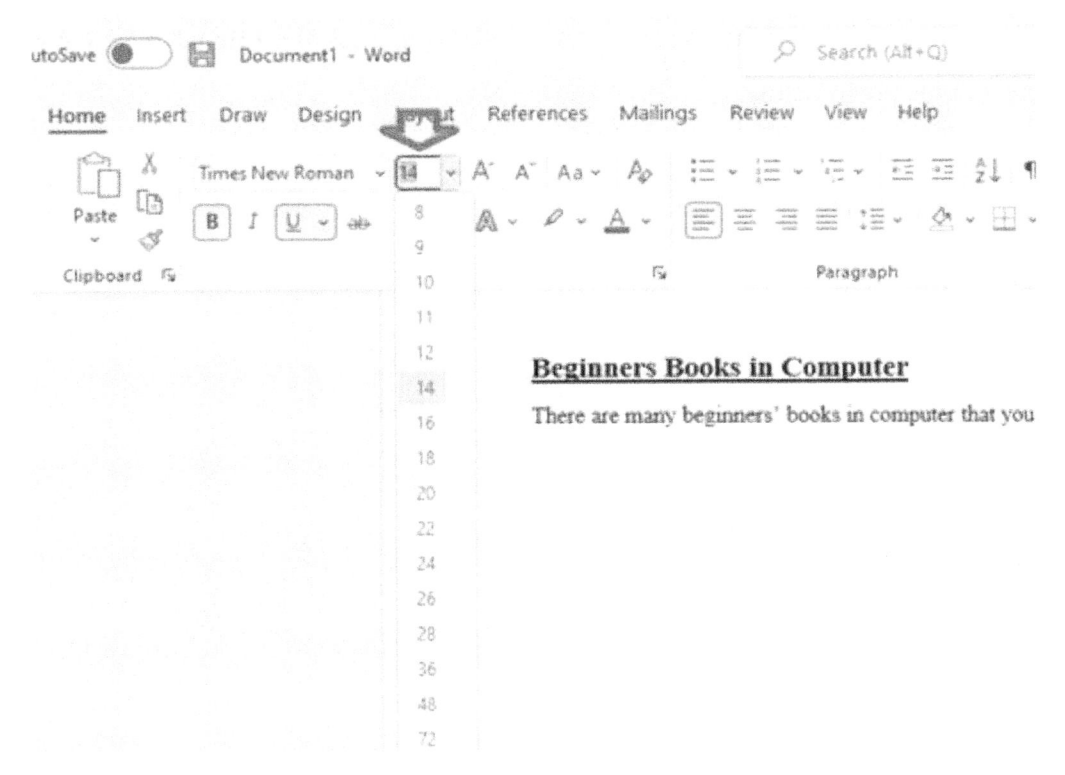

About to choose new font size

So, select any font size and you will see the change it will make on the text in return. Irrespective of the font size you choose at the moment, you can change it to another size if you are not okay with the one you selected.

How to Save a Document
Without saving the document you created using Microsoft Word app, all the time you spent typing will be a waste. So, it is important you carefully save your document. After saving the document you created, you can open it anytime you want to use it. I was able to publish this book you are reading because I saved the document. It is a work that took time to complete, but all I was doing was that anytime I finished any part, I saved the document to continue later. I was doing this until I finished the composition of the document.

To save any document, the first step you are to take is to click the **File** tab. The tab is illustrated in the photo below.

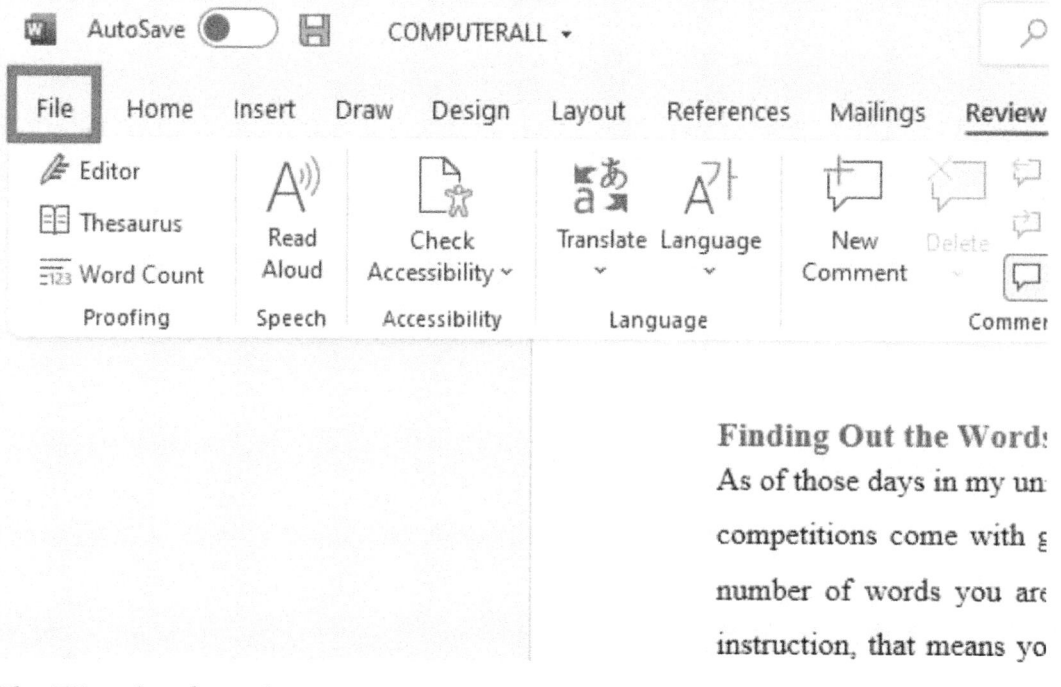

*The **File** tab indicated*

You will see some options, select **Save As** followed by **This PC**.

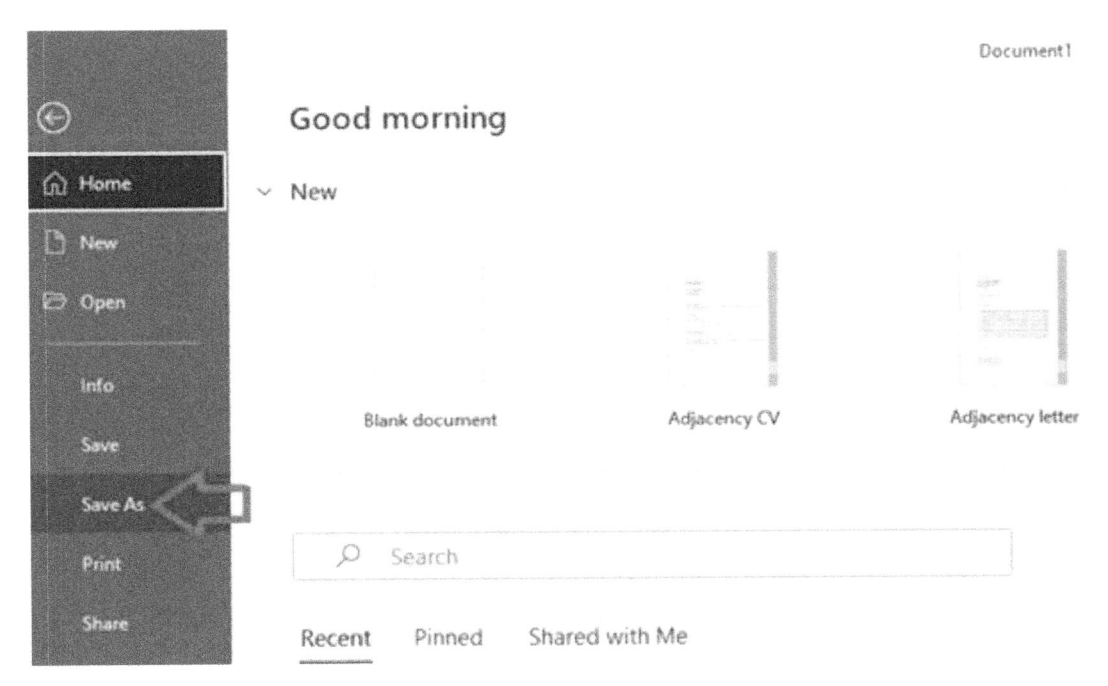

*The **Save as** command indicated*

A location of your computer will open automatically. Navigate to the folder where you want the document to be saved. Give the file a name of your choice, example "computer document".

And lastly, click the **Save** button for the document to be saved. As an added information, irrespective of the fact that you have saved the document, as you type on the document later, after few minutes click on the **Save** icon that is top left-hand corner or just press the keyboard shortcut keys **Ctrl + S** to save your newly added contents in the document. I explained this under the **Working Smart in Your Document** subheading.

How to Print a Document
Sometimes, after composing your document, you may like to have it in hardcopy. As a result of that, you need to print the document. It is very possible in Microsoft Word app.

To print the document, click the **File** tab. Scroll down the page and then select **Print** command. The print command is indicated in the photo below.

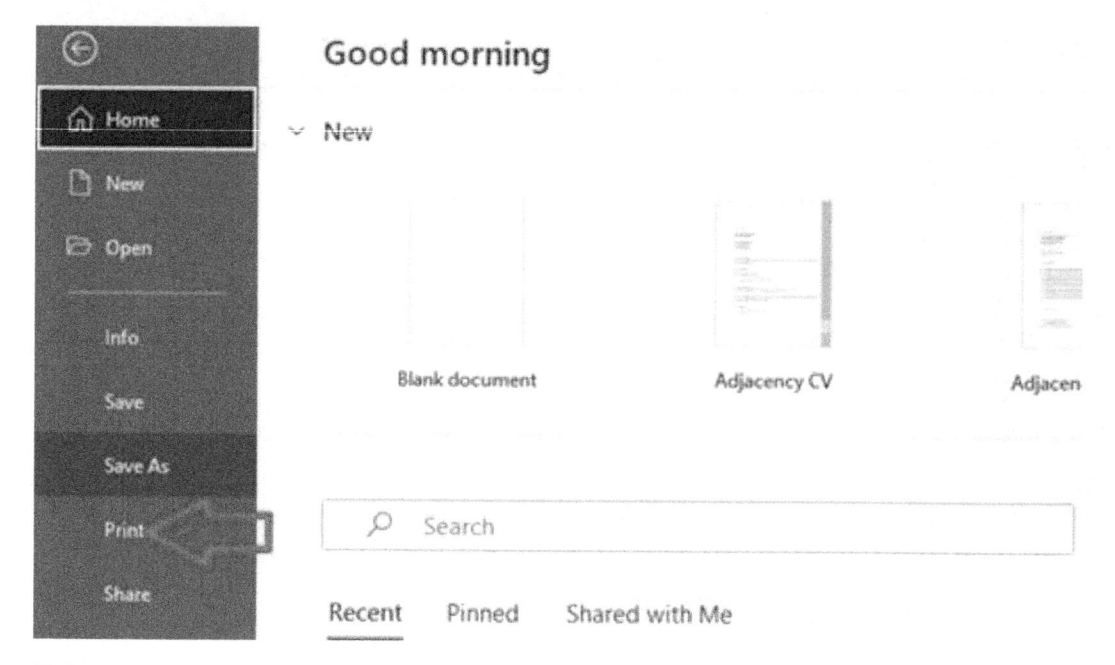

Print *command indicated for printing process*

The next step you are to take is to set how you want the document printed. And lastly, hit the **Print** button for the document to be printed.

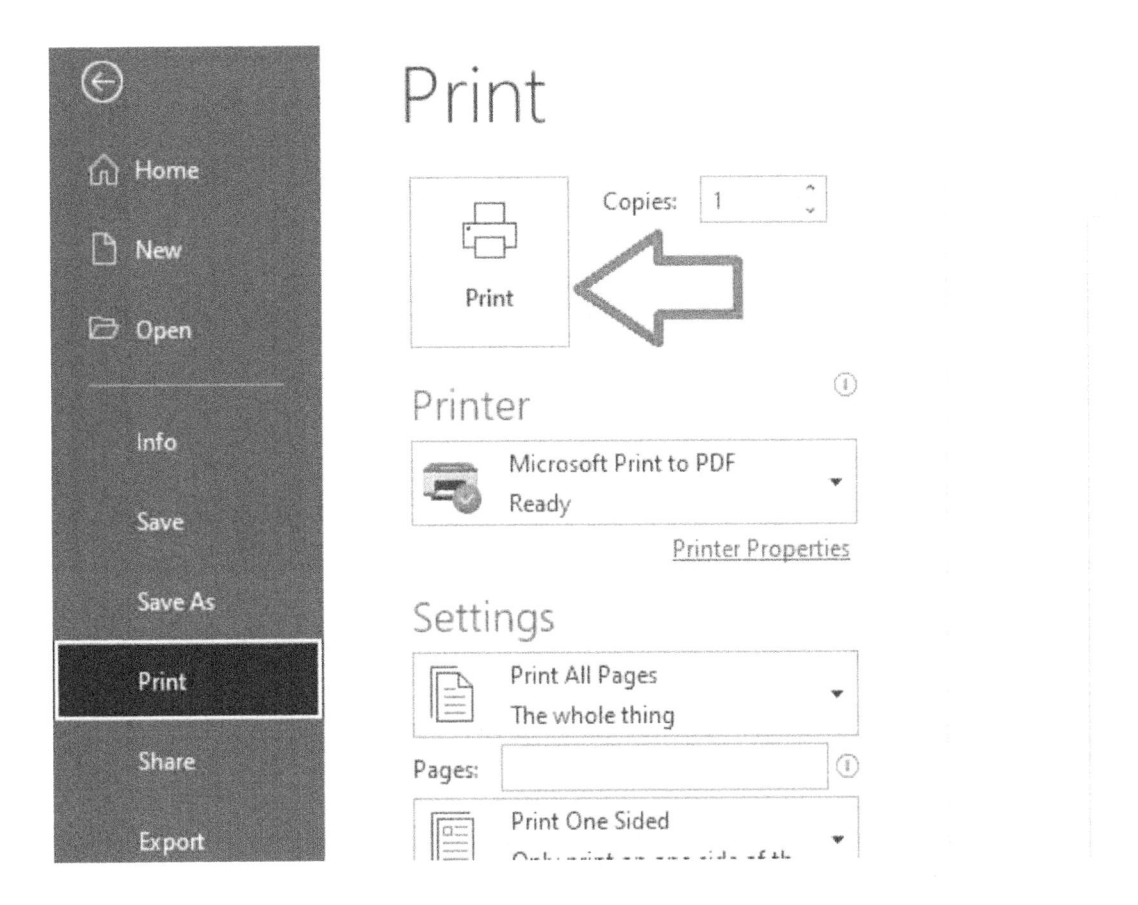

*The **Print** button indicated*

Ensure your computer is connected to a printer which is powered on before you start the printing process.

When you are done printing or working on your word document, close the Microsoft Word app. To close the app, just click on the **close icon** which is indicated in the photo below.

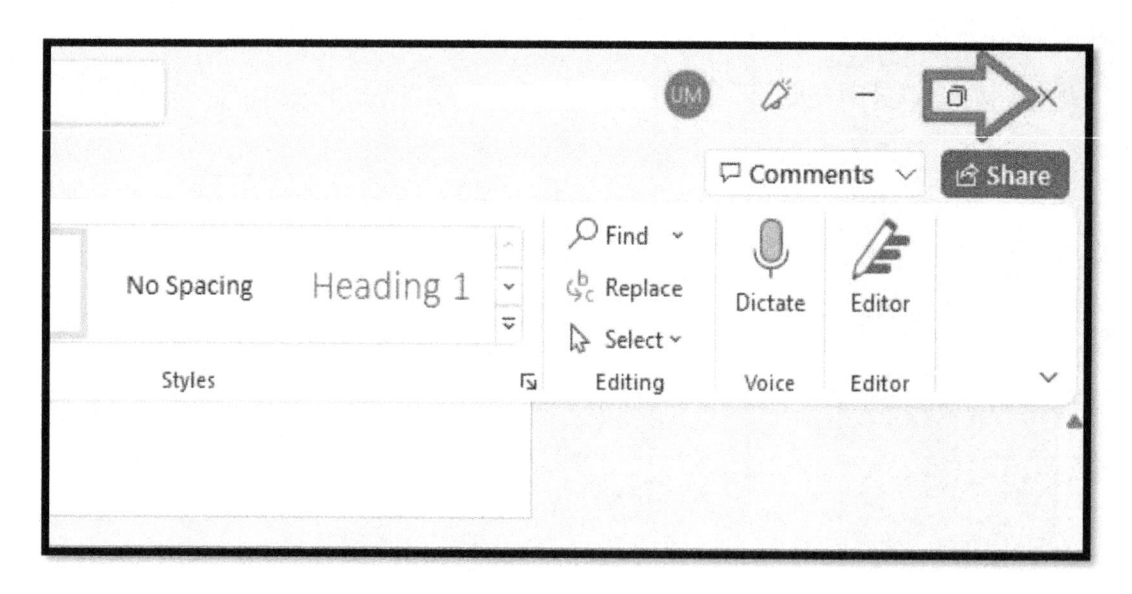

*The **Close icon** pointed by the arrow (positioned at the top right-hand side of Word interface)*

As a beginner or a senior, this information on Microsoft Word presented here is enough to get you started on how to use Microsoft Word on your computer. Let's proceed to Excel in the next chapter. You learn more to gain more, and in return grow your knowledge on computer.

CHAPTER 5

GUIDE ON MICROSOFT EXCEL

Microsoft Excel which is often called "Excel" is one of the most used spreadsheet program all over the world. It is an app used mainly for calculations, comparing, graphing and in data analysis. If you have been in a business conference or meeting where charts are used to analyse information, that chart might have been created with Excel app. If an organization has over 1,000 employees for instance and the manager wants the names of the employees prepared in a spreadsheet document, Excel app does the job well.

If you are someone who wants to find yourself in an office one day working as an employee, the knowledge of Excel is likely to be required from you. So, if you want to stand out from the crowd on the day of the interview, you need to have the knowledge of Excel. Having the basic knowledge on Excel will keep you up and running. But, if you want to learn Excel to the core, you may consider buying the book I wrote on it only.

The title of the book is "EXCEL 2022: Essentials Skill Guide on Microsoft Excel for Beginners and Seniors with Illustrations Plus Charts, Formulas and Practical Exercises" by KASPER B. LANGMAN

The author's book on Excel

At the beginning of this book, I walked you through on how you can install Microsoft 365 app on your computer. I went further to explain that on the installation of the Microsoft 365 software on your computer, your computer will have some major office apps which include Microsoft Word and Excel. So, if you followed that guide properly, I believe you will have Excel app in your computer right now. But if you already have this app installed in your computer which may not be Excel 365 version, you are still good to go. I will walk you through on how to use the app without stress.

Excel Terms

There are some terms we use in Excel. Getting yourself acquainted with these terms will make you a good user of the software. Also, it will make you to flow easily as I go deep in letting you know more on this chapter on Excel. Let's get it rolling.

Tabs

Tabs are different menus, which you will see when you launch your Excel app and select blank workbook or any template of your choice. They are at the top part of the Excel spreadsheet interface. When I get into practical teaching on this area of interest, I will be mentioning some tabs like Home, Insert, File and the rest. Irrespective of the version of Excel you are using on your computer, they are all built with different tabs.

Ribbons

When you select any tab of your choice from which you can complete a task or tasks in Excel, you will see ribbons. The term ribbons are commands that are created under each tab of Excel app. Sometimes, commands are used in the place of ribbons. So, whether I use ribbon or command, know that I am referring to the same thing. In addition, ribbons are grouped. An example of a ribbon inside Home tab is **Bold**. And the Bold is classified in **Fonts** group.

Spreadsheet

A spreadsheet is that work environment of an Excel app where data are entered and analysed. If you are plotting graph, that graph is also plotted on a spreadsheet as well. Without spreadsheet, there is nothing like Excel app. Spreadsheet is also called sheet in short form.

Workbook

Each of the sheet creates a workbook. Breaking it further, a workbook can be defined as the summation of all sheets created using an Excel app. A workbook can have different departments of sheets.

Columns

In Excel, columns are the vertical order that are denoted with Alphabetical letters. They run from top to down. The order of the letters is A, B, C, D, and so on.

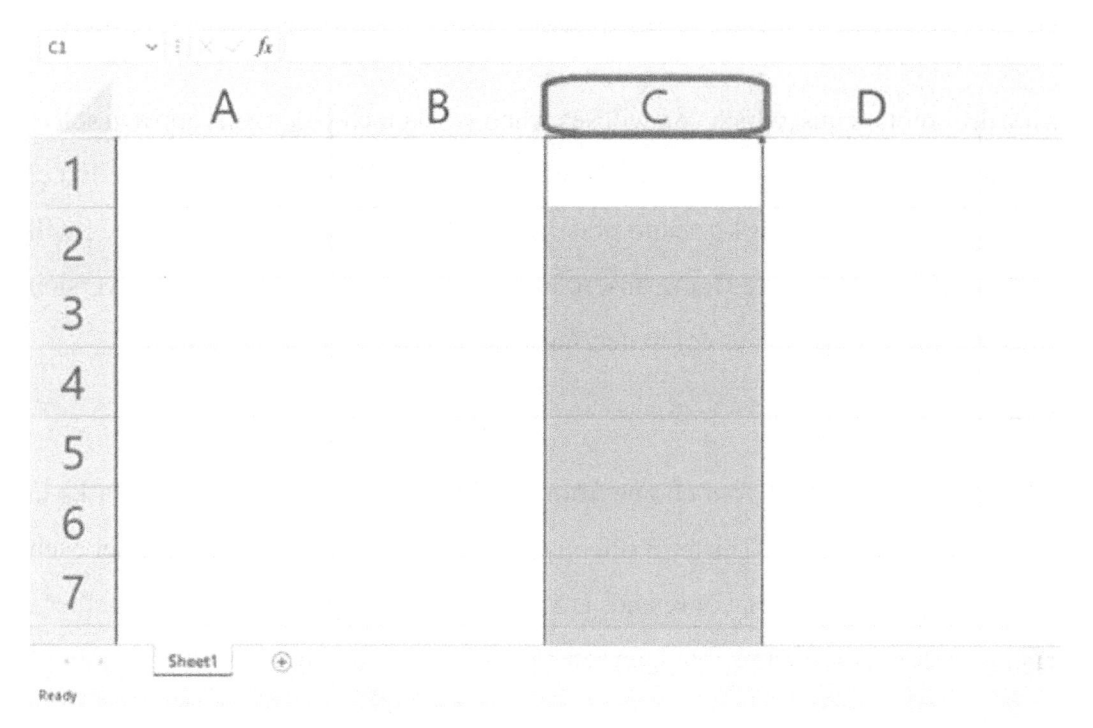

Photo illustrates Column C

Note: In the above photo, I zoomed the spreadsheet and that is the reason it appeared bolder that the default size. To zoom a spreadsheet, drag the Zoom line at the bottom left-hand corner forward.

Rows

In a spreadsheet, the rows complement the columns. They run horizontally and they are numbered. They are numbered from 1, 2, 3, 4 and so on. The numbers are properly arranged in a way that users of the program can use them to complete the naming of cells.

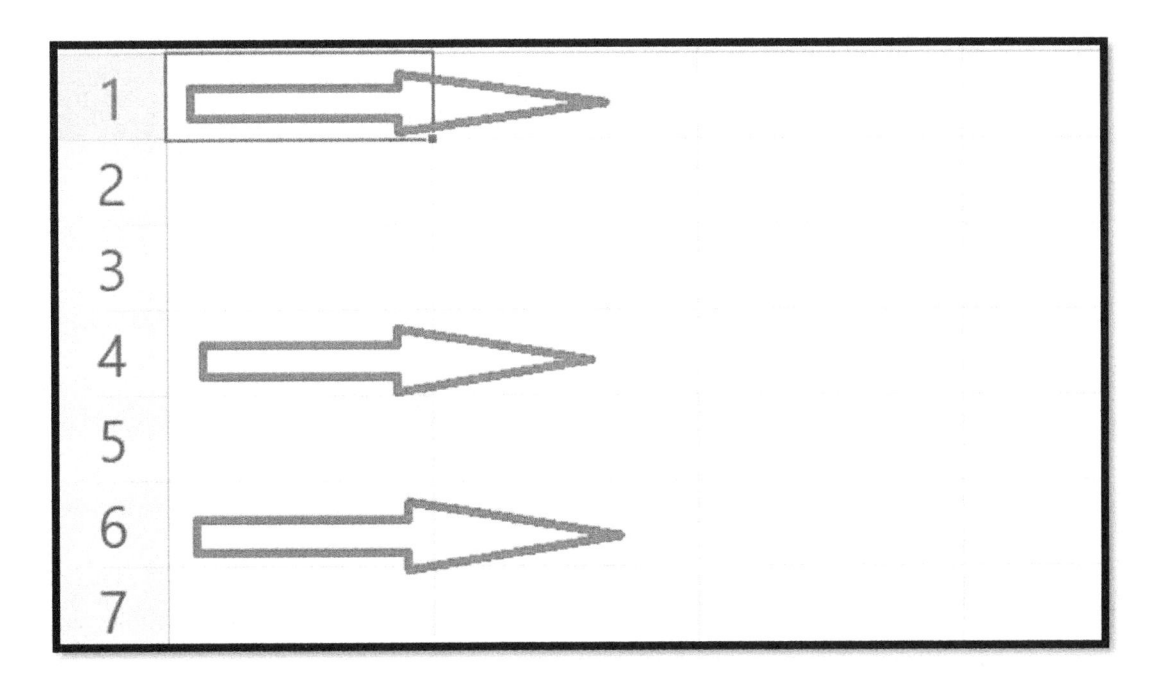

Photo illustrates the direction of a row

Cells

The interception of columns and rows produce cells. They are the small rectangle shapes that make the spreadsheet of an Excel. They are the building blocks of a sheet. As I stated before, it is the crosses between the rows and columns that produce cells. When you see information like cell A1. What that means is that it is the interception of column A and row 1 that forms the cell.

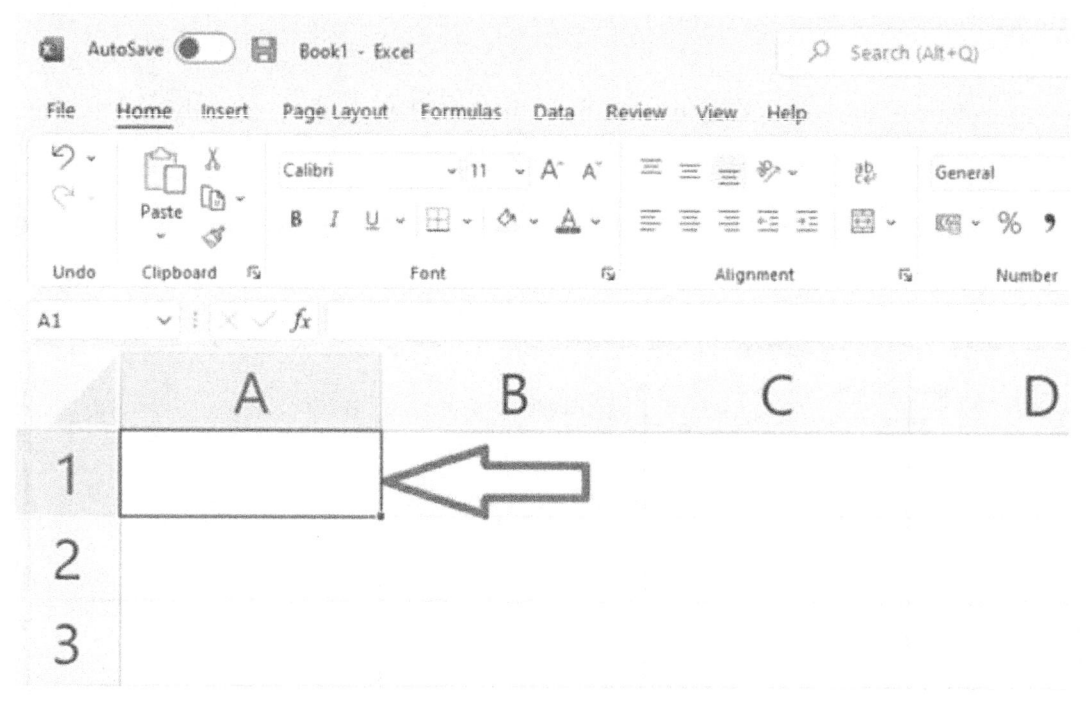

Cell A1 indicated in the photo

Launching Excel App for the First Time

Before you can work in Excel, you need to launch. By launching the app, I mean you need to open the app first. So, to open an Excel app, click on the Excel icon if it is pinned at the taskbar of your computer for it to be launched. But, if it is not pinned at the taskbar section of your computer, you then need to search for it in your computer and then click for it to be launched.

To search for the App in your computer, click the **Search** icon pinned at the taskbar of your computer, and then type the text "Excel" in the search bar just as you can see in the photo below.

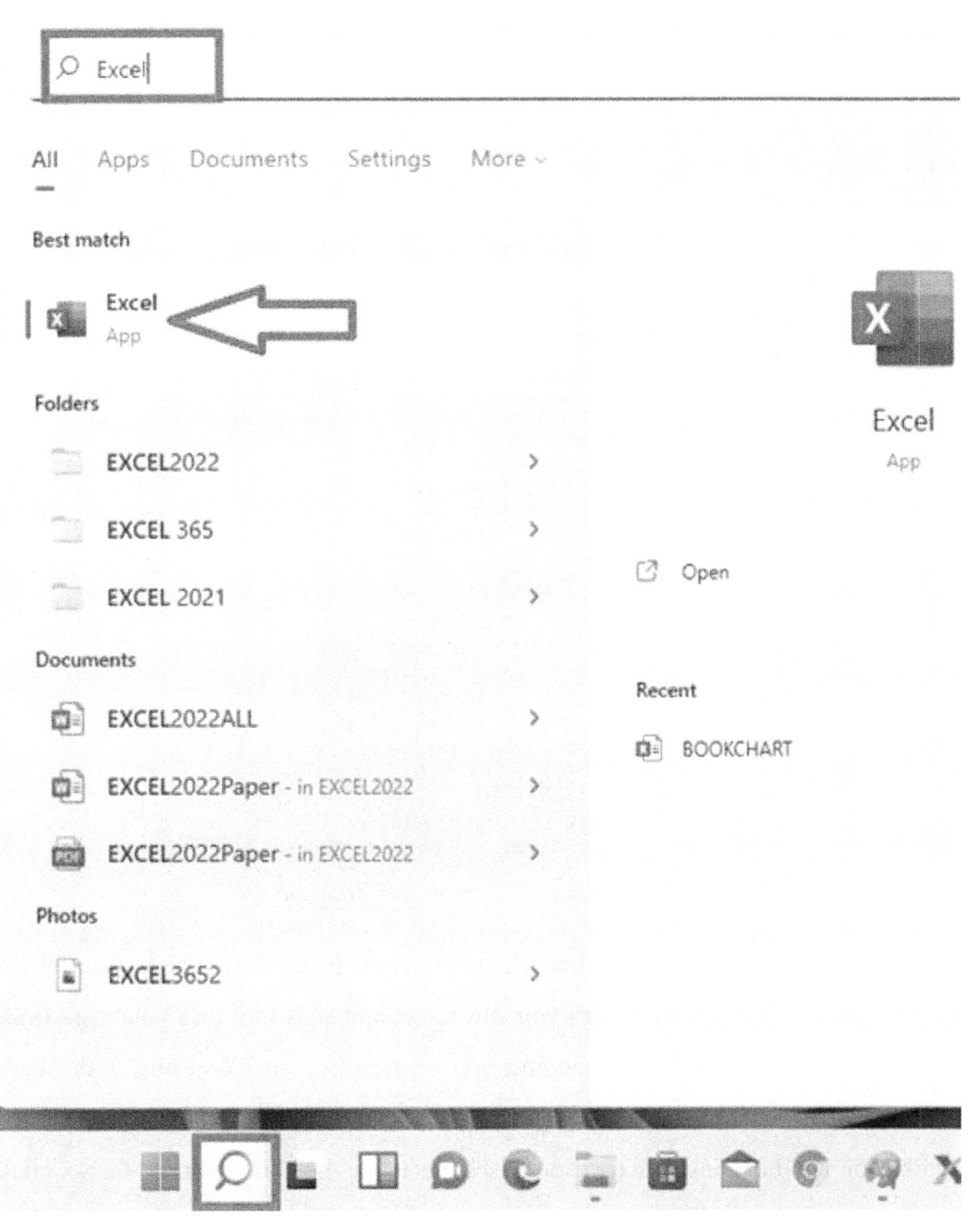

About to launch an Excel app by first searching for it using Search icon

As the Excel app shows up the search result just as you can see in the above photo, click on it and it will open. As it opens, below is the first page you will see.

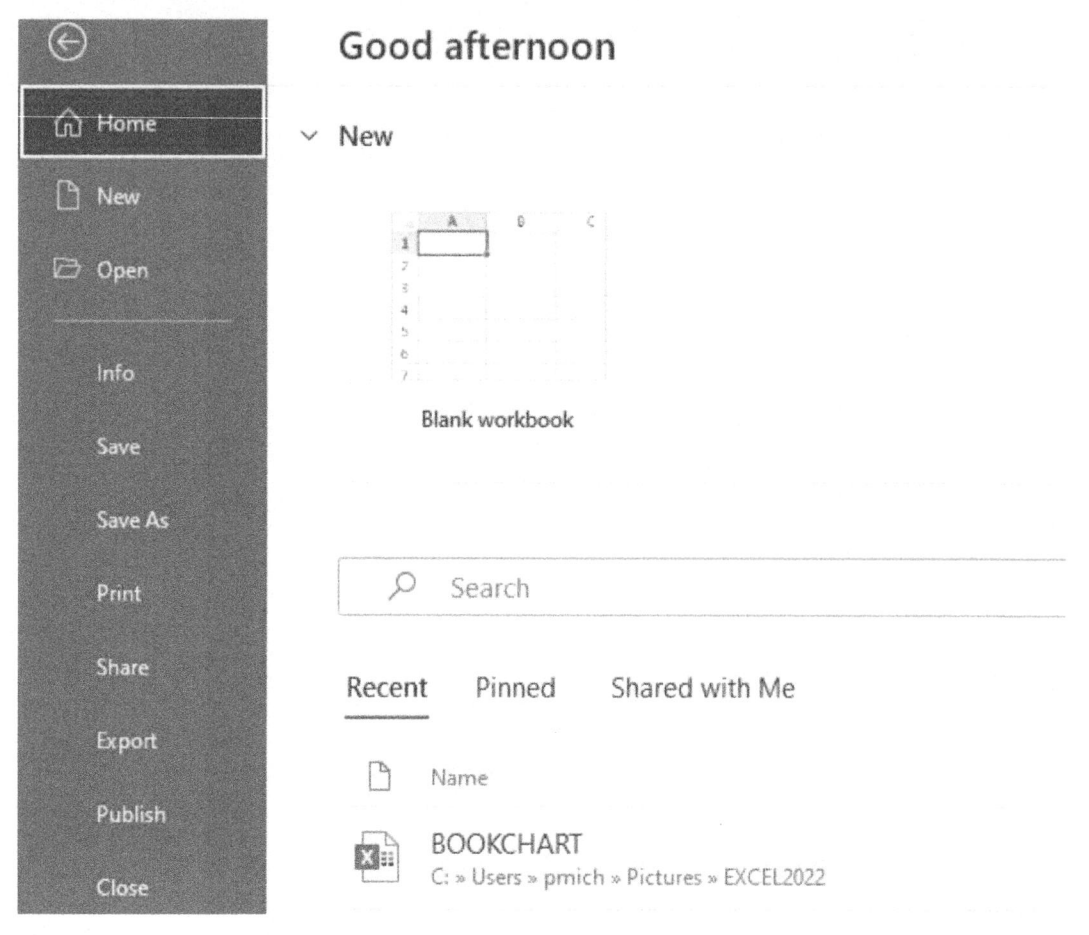

The first page that appears when I launched my Excel 365 app

Looking at the above photo, sometimes when the Excel app gets launched, you will see Blank workbook and other templates you can select and start building your data from there. In this teaching, I will be teaching you on how to use Excel app with blank workbook. So, no need to start thinking too much on Excel templates. In fact, 99% of the works you will be doing in Excel spreadsheet is using the blank workbook. So, click on the **Blank workbook** for it to open. As it opens, you will see the workbook interface with some tabs and commands (that is ribbons).

Knowing Excel Tabs

If you are using recent Excel versions like Excel 365 or Excel 2021, when you select Blank workbook and the spreadsheet opens fully, you will see the tabs that are built into the platform. If you are using certain versions of Excel that are not too old, these tabs are also there. Tabs of Excel 365 version are indicated in the photo below.

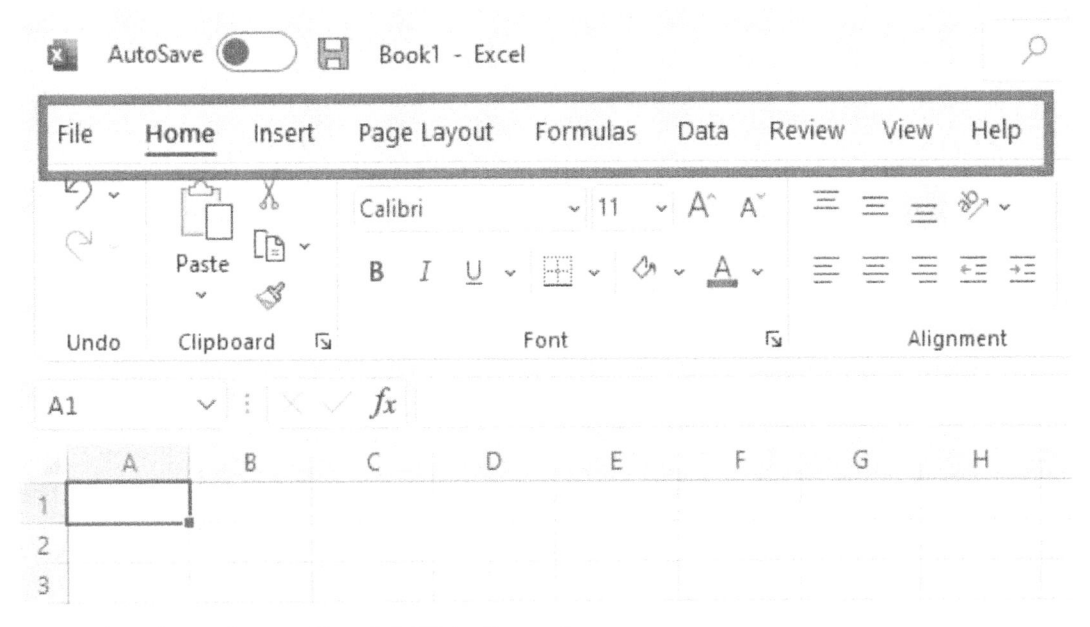

The tabs of Excel app (Excel 365) indicated

Taking a good look at the above photo, the tabs of the spreadsheet are File, Home, Insert, Page Layout, Formulas, Data, Review, View and Help. When you click on any tab, it opens ribbons.

How to Enter Data in a Spreadsheet

To enter any data in the cell of a spreadsheet, the first step you are to take is to click on that cell and then start typing. When you are done typing, click on another cell, you can continue entering other data in the other cell.

Sometimes, beginners want to edit the text they entered in a cell but end up deleting the former data once they click on the cell and start typing. When you click on a cell and start typing, what was there initially is replaced with the new text. But, to get in a cell, double-click on it and then with the help of arrow key make the changes you need.

	A	B	C	D
1	CLASSES	NUMBER		
2	Class A	28		
3	Class B	20		
4	Class C	32		
5				

A spreadsheet with some data in different cells

How to Make Text Bold in Excel
Sometimes, there is need to make some text that you typed in cells bold. The information in those cells may be the headings of the spreadsheet so you need to make them bold to differentiate them from the rest cells of the spreadsheet.

To make any text bold, select the cell that contains the text by just clicking on it. The next step you are to take is to click the **Home** tab. Bold is one of the ribbons in the Home tab, so, click the **Bold icon.**

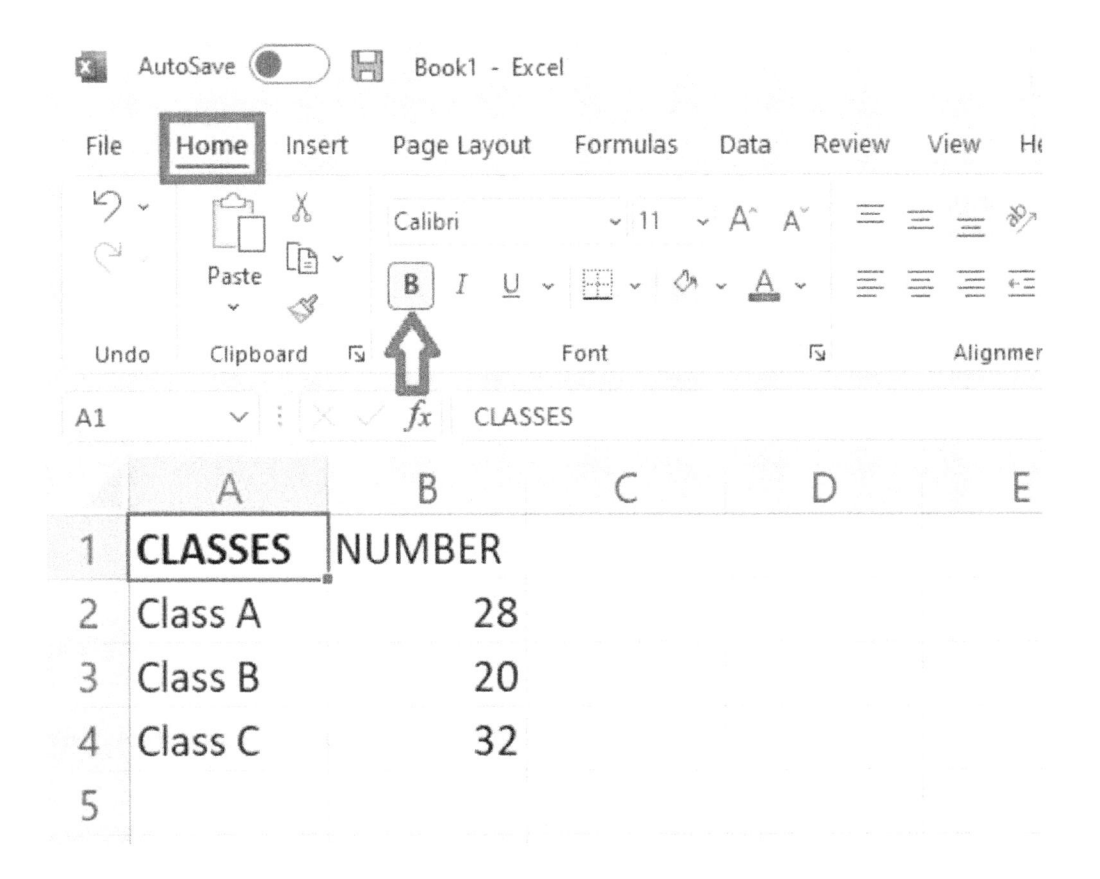

	A	B
1	**CLASSES**	NUMBER
2	Class A	28
3	Class B	20
4	Class C	32
5		

The Bold icon of Excel indicated

Immediately you take this last step, the text in that cell will become bold.

How to Extend a Cell in Excel
There will be some occasions when it will look as if the words you type in a cell extends into another cell close to it. It is just an illusion, but it is important you make the necessary adjustment. So, place your mouse between the two column letters (on the line) to obtain the double-sided arrow design just as you can see in the photo below.

	A	B	C
1	CLASSES	NUMBER	
2	Class A	28	
3	Class B	20	
4	Class C	32	

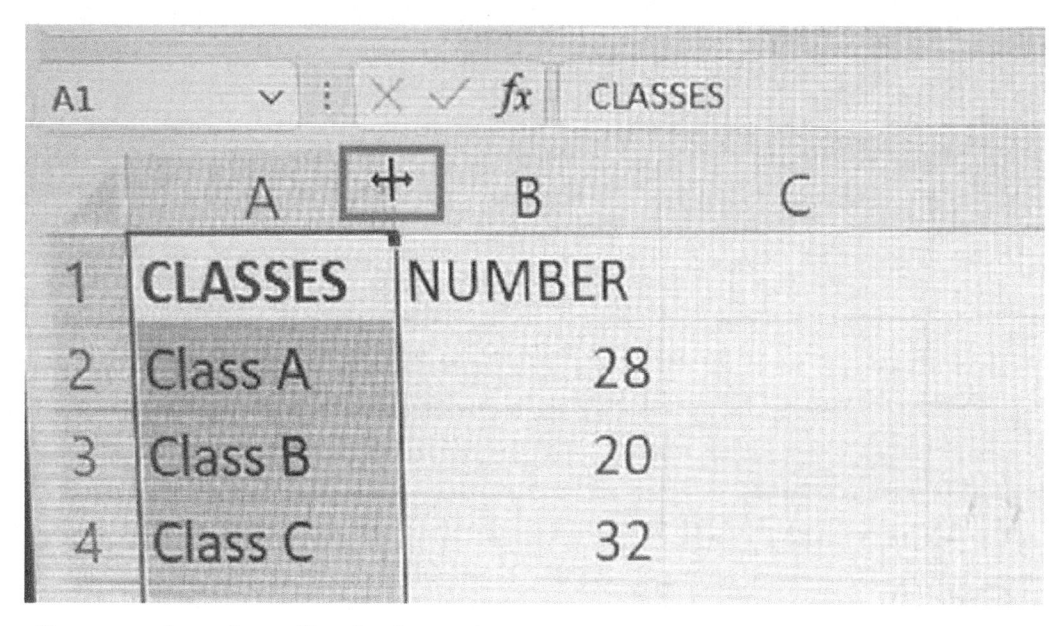

About to adjust the cells of column A

Once you see the double-sided arrow design, press the left mouse button of your computer and drag towards the right for the cell to be extended. Once you get the desired size, release the pressure on the left mouse button. Use this approach to adjust any cell in Excel.

Changing Text Color in Excel
You can decide to change the text color of some words you have in your workbook to make that part stand out from others. You can apply unique text color to the headings you have in your Excel spreadsheet.

To change text color, select the cell that has the text you want to change its color. The next step is for you to click the **Home** tab. Click on the **Font color** command and select the color of your choice.

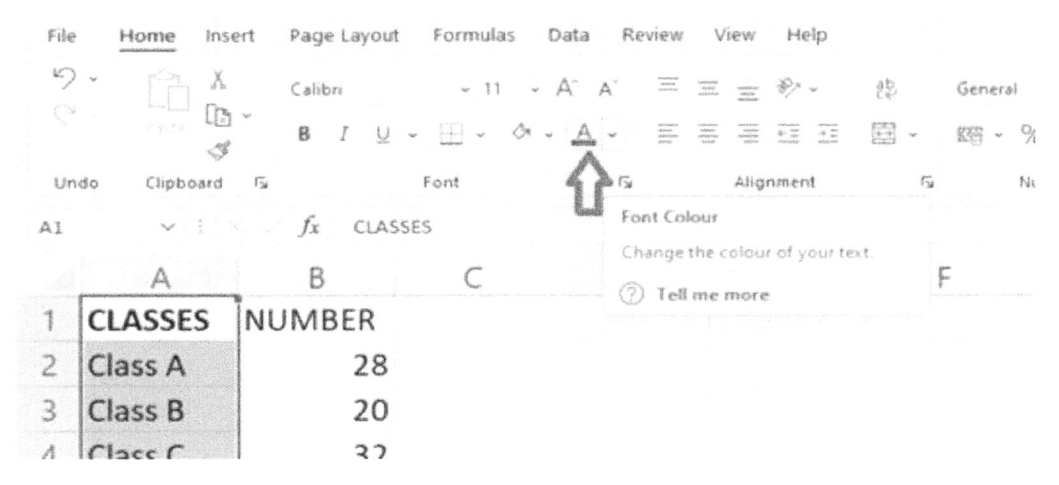

About to change font color

Immediately you select the color you want to change the font to, it is applied. These are the simple steps to change font color in Microsoft Excel.

Selecting Spreadsheet Data
If you want to select the entire workbook you are working on, press the keyboard shortcut **Ctrl** + **A** on your computer keyboard. But if you want to select a range of your workbook, select the first cell where you want to start the selection by just a click. Then drag towards the right or left depending on the position of the other cells you want to select, and they will be selected.

Creating More than One Sheet in a Workbook
When you launch an Excel app and then select Blank workbook, the workbook opens with just one sheet inside. You can add more than one sheet in workbook. This usually applies when different segments are required in one workbook. Take for instance you are given an assignment to prepare data showing major companies in a small city with the names of their employees. In a situation like this, it will be more organized if each company data is composed in one sheet of a workbook.

To add more than one spreadsheet in a workbook, click the enclosed + sign at the bottom left of the workbook.

The enclosed + icon indicated

When you click that icon, a new sheet is added. Use this approach to add as many sheets as you want in a workbook.

Merging Cells of a Spreadsheet
Let me assume you are composing names of students in a particular class of a school. In that workbook where the names are prepared, the workbook is given a heading like "NAMES OF STUDENTS IN CLASS A". When you type such heading, it is likely to look as if the heading cuts into the next cells close to the one you started from just as seen in the photo below.

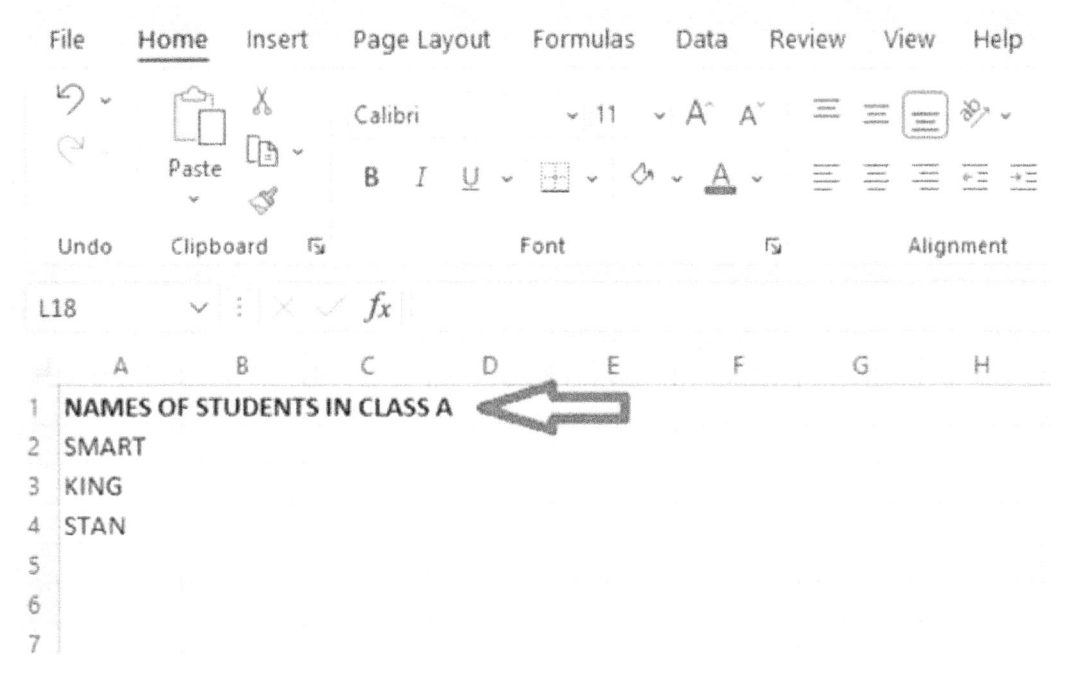

The heading of a workbook with text that extends to other cells

To sort this challenge so that all the text will enter in a single cell, you need to merge the cell you started from with the others it extends to. So, to merge the cells, select the cells first. The next step is to click the **Home** tab.

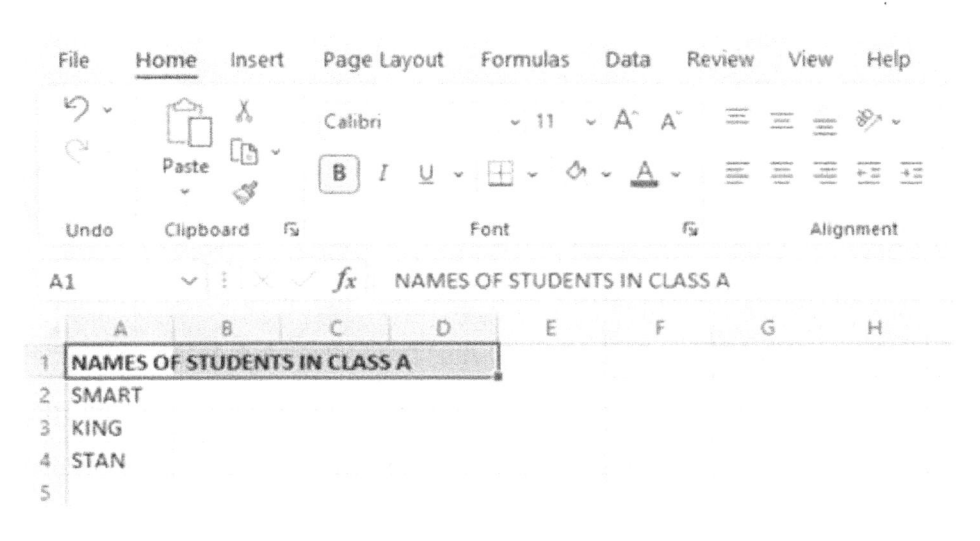

About to merge cells to form a unit

And lastly, click the **Merge & Center** button and the cell will form a unit.

143

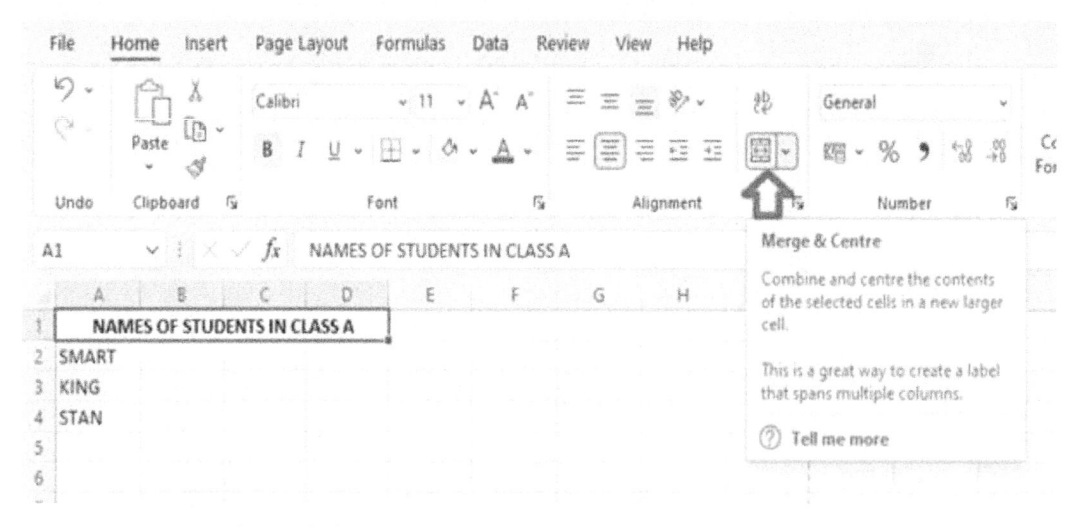

The result after the cells have been merged

Plotting Charts in Excel

Charts are ways to analyze the data you have in a spreadsheet. Sometimes, it creates visual understanding of the point you are trying to pass to your audience. With Excel app, you can create different types of charts. The charts you can create on Excel spreadsheet are many including Pie chart, column chart, bar chart, sunburst, line chart, scatter plot, and so many others.

In this subheading, I will guide you on how you can create a sample chart on Excel spreadsheet. Once you understand this sample chart, you can create any other chart type on your own. I will be creating a column chart.

The first step you are to take is to prepare your data. Let me assume that you are a teacher in one primary school. The primary school runs from Class A to D. The principal of the school gave you instruction to prepare a data showing these classes and the number of students in each class. After preparation of the data using a spreadsheet, the information below is what you have.

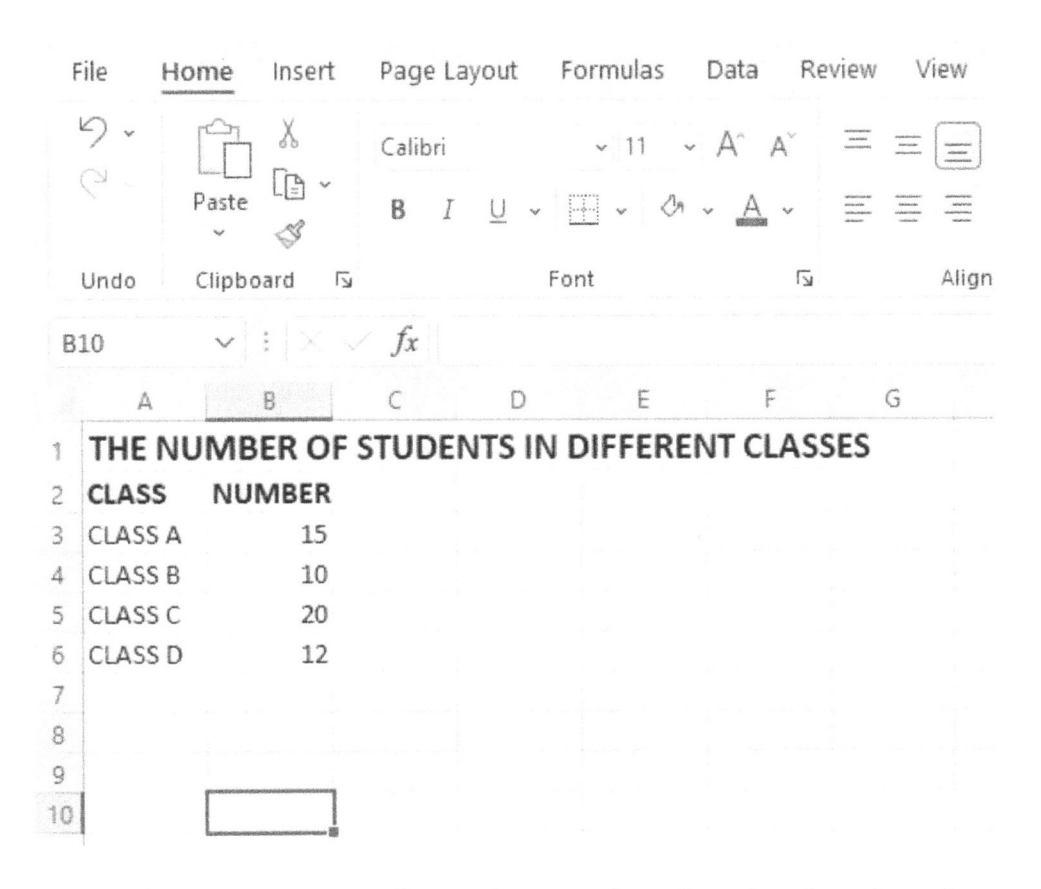

A spreadsheet containing different classes and number of students in each

To represent the above data in a column chart, select the entire data. The photo below is the screenshot of the data after they are selected.

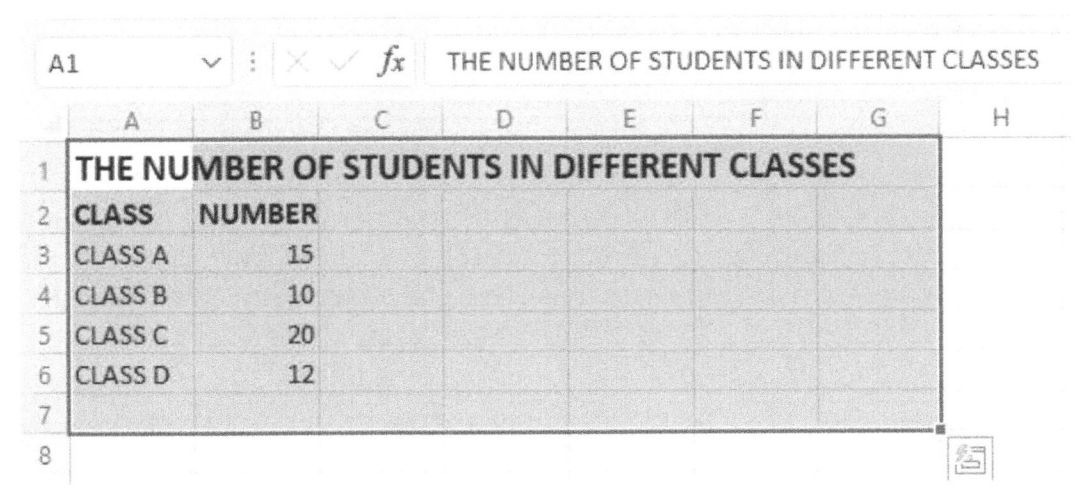

Selected data to be represented in a column chart

Click the **Insert** tab and some ribbons will be displayed. The next step is for you to click the **Recommended charts** ribbon.

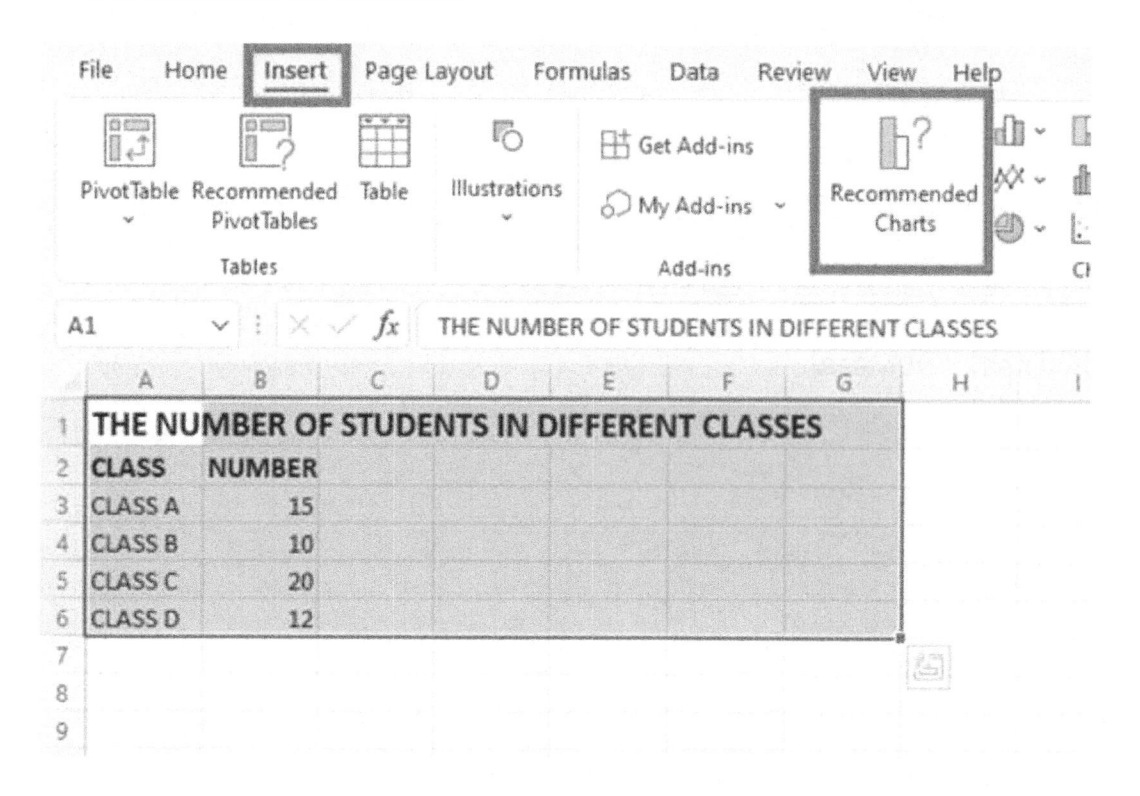

*The **Insert** tab and **Recommended charts** ribbon indicated*

On clicking on the **Recommended charts**, charts dialog box will show up. On the dialog box, click the **All charts** heading. The next step to take is to click **Column** chart option.

*The **All charts** heading, and **Column** chart indicated*

You will see some designs of column chart. Just select any design you want to insert on the spreadsheet and click the **OK** button. As soon as you take this last step, the chart is inserted on the workbook. You can drag it to any part of the workbook you want to have it.

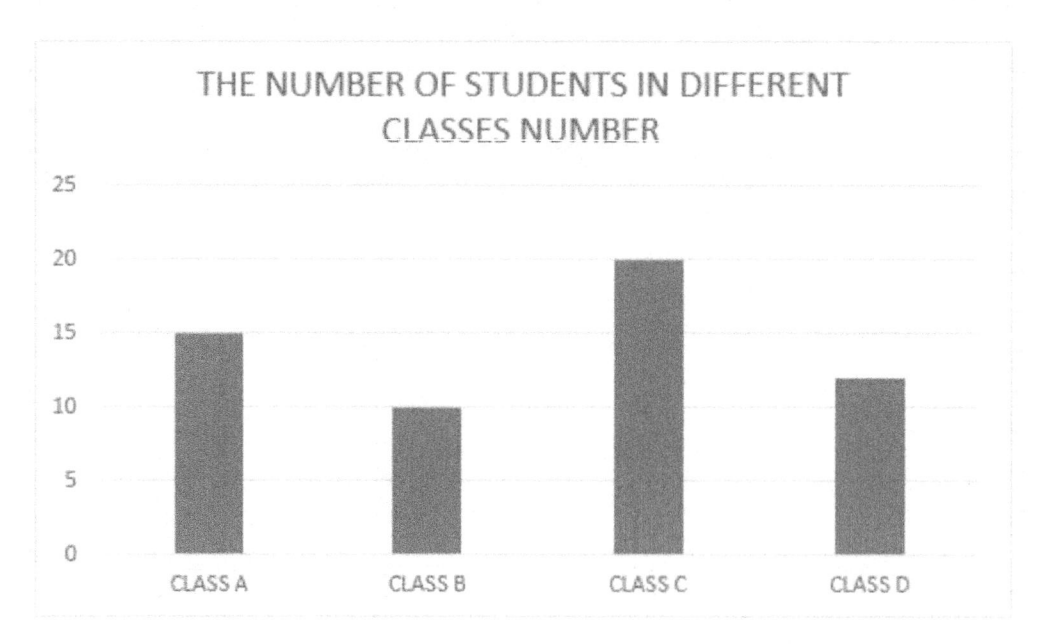

Plotted column chart

Printing in Excel

Many beginners and seniors do not know that it is possible to print the data they prepared in Excel spreadsheet. It is very possible just like the way I taught you how to print Word document in chapter 4.

You can print the part that contain the data you prepared on the sheet (it is called a range) or the entire spreadsheet. But, in most cases, range is printed because it is of no importance printing any blank document that has no information on it.

To print the part of the spreadsheet that has some information on it, take these steps:

Select the data on the spreadsheet which you want to print, just as you can see in the photo below.

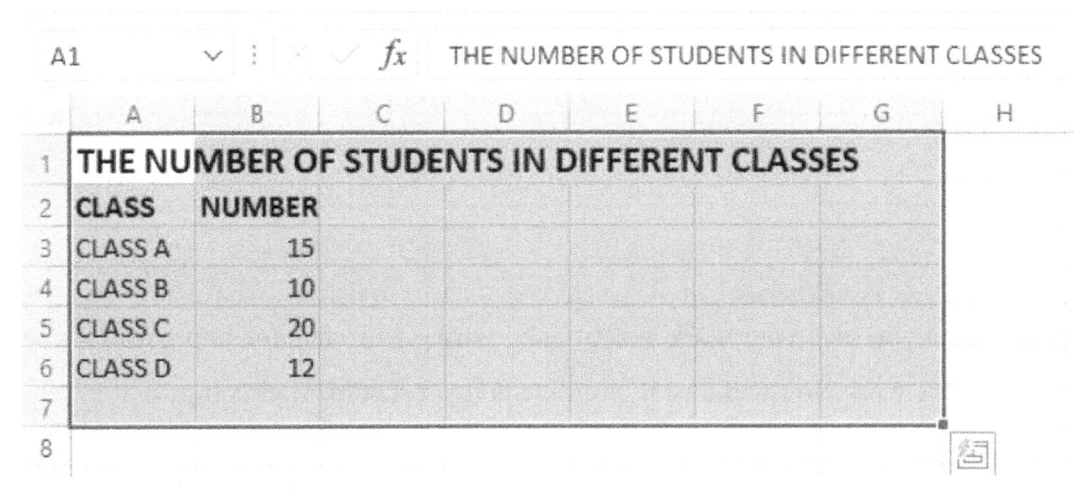

	A	B	C	D	E	F	G	H
1	THE NUMBER OF STUDENTS IN DIFFERENT CLASSES							
2	CLASS	NUMBER						
3	CLASS A	15						
4	CLASS B	10						
5	CLASS C	20						
6	CLASS D	12						
7								
8								

About to print a range of the spreadsheet

Click the **File** tab, and from the list of commands select **Print.** On the next page that will be displayed, click the **Print** button which is indicated in the photo below.

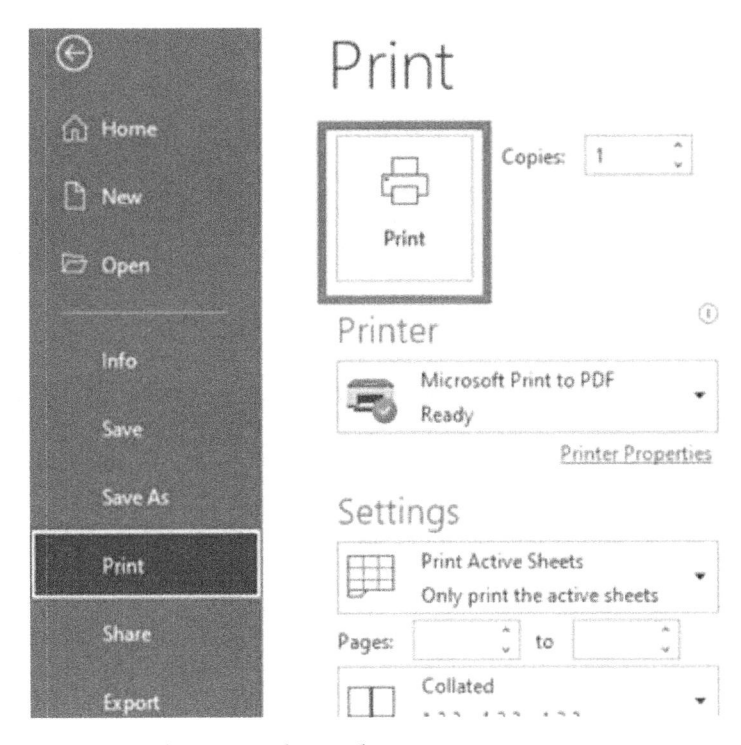

*The **Print** button indicated*

Once you take the last step, exercise a little patience and the spreadsheet document will be printed out from the printer.

Note: Before you start the printing, make sure your printer is properly connected to your computer. Also, if you want to print more than one copy, type the number in the space for **Copies**.

How to Save a Workbook

It is important you save your workbook after preparing your data for future use. If you do not save the work, you will lose it. So, save your workbook after composing it.

To save a workbook, click the **File** tab of your Excel first. The next step is to click the **Save As** command. From the options you will see, select **Browse** for a location to open in your computer.

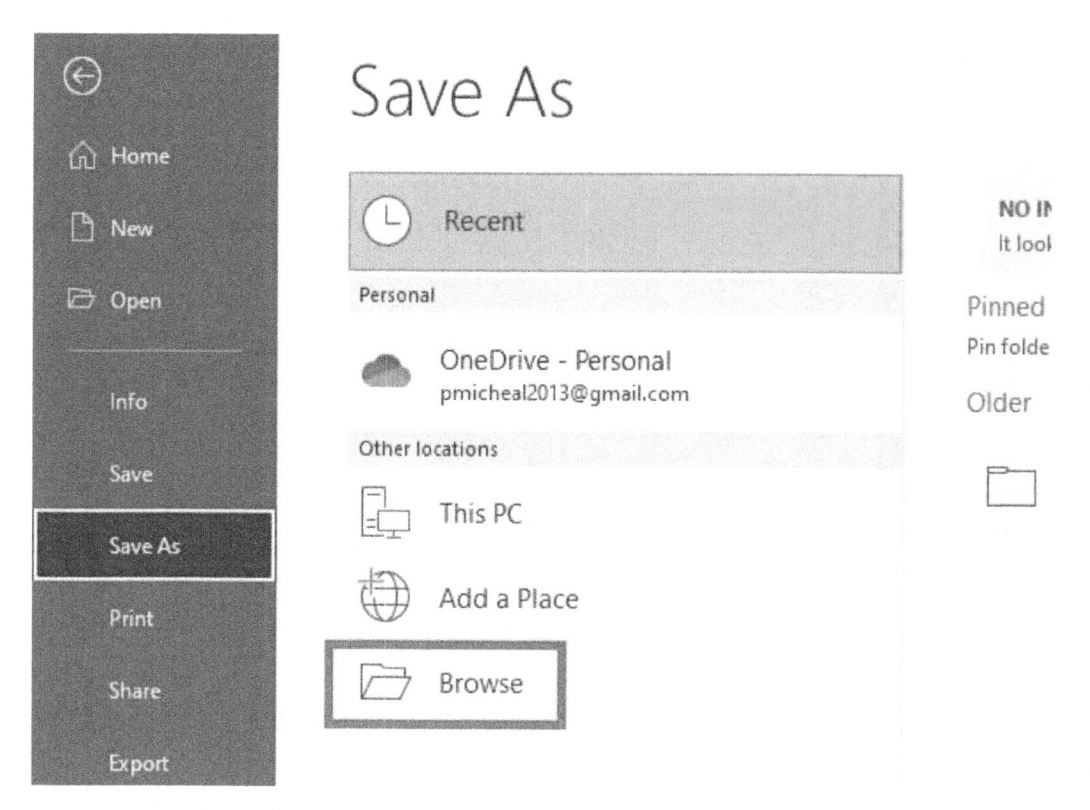

Progress in saving a workbook

Double-click on any folder where you want to save the file. In the space for **File name**, type the name you want the workbook to be identified with. In the space for **Save as**

type, leave it at **Excel Workbook**. And lastly, click the **Save** button for the file to be saved.

Anytime you want to access this file again, click the **File Explorer** icon pinned at the taskbar of your computer. Locate the folder where you saved the file and double-click on it. When the folder opens, double-click on the workbook file for it to open.

APPRECIATION
Thank you for the time spent in reading this book.

INDEX

A

add pictures, 117
All Apps, 52, 53

B

Blank document, 114
Blank workbook, 136, 141
bookmark, 94

C

CAPITALIZE, 117
character keys, 26, 27, 65
Charts, iv, 129, 144
computer terminology, 4, 23
copy, 13, 34, 79, 83, 84, 100, 111, 150
CPU, 6, 8
Ctrl + S, 115, 125
Cut, iii, 83, 84

D

desktop, 21, 46, 47, 48, 50, 66, 70, 73, 74, 78, 111
Documents, 78, 79, 80, 81
Do-It-Yourself, 1

E

Edge, 6, 55, 61, 72, 79, 91, 92, 93, 94, 96, 97, 98, 100, 102, 109
email, 20, 58, 61, 102, 104, 106, 107, 109
Excel, iv, 4, 55, 59, 60, 67, 76, 77, 111, 128, 129, 130, 131, 132, 133, 134, 135, 136, 137, 138, 139, 140, 141, 144, 148, 150, 151

F

File Explorer, 7, 62, 63, 72, 73, 77, 78, 79, 80, 109, 151
Flight mode icon, 87
Focus Assist, iii, 87, 88

H

Hardware, 4
Hibernate, 10

I

internet connection, 18, 34, 38, 57, 65, 87

L

launch, 51, 54, 57, 63, 65, 91, 112, 113, 131, 134, 135, 141

M

means, *i*
Merge & Center, 143
Microsoft 365, 60, 61, 62, 63, 67, 111, 131
Microsoft Store, 55, 56, 57, 58, 59, 73
Microsoft Word, iii, 4, 14, 27, 29, 30, 31, 55, 59, 60, 63, 67, 69, 75, 111, 112, 114, 116, 121, 124, 125, 127, 128, 131
modem, 44, 45, 65

N

new folder, 49
new sheet, 142
number keys, 26

O

output devices, 13, 14

P

paste, 78, 83, 84, 100
Pin to taskbar, 77, 97
Print button, 126, 127, 149
Priority only, 87

R

RAM, 5, 11
Ribbons, 131

153

S

saving, 79, 88, 124, 150
screen brightness, 84
search bar, 5, 68, 76, 112, 134
setup, 15, 16, 18, 19, 20, 21, 24, 46, 55, 60, 78, 104, 109
Shut down, 9, 10
Sleep, 9, 10
smartphones, 34, 35
Software, 4
Spacebar, 27, 65
special character keys, 26
Spreadsheet, iv, 131, 132, 137, 141, 142

T

Tabs, 131, 136, 137

taskbar section, 66, 76, 85, 134
This PC, 7, 8, 109, 125

U

USB tethering, 38, 44, 65

V

Virtual desktop, 70
Volume, iii, 84, 85, 88, 89

W

Wi-Fi, ii, 35, 36
Windows computers, 1, 3, 15, 65
Windows logo icon, 51, 52, 54, 66
Word count, 121

Made in the USA
Las Vegas, NV
11 August 2022